PRAISE F(
THE SECRET POWER OF KINDNESS

"I'm sure that there must be books out there devoted exclusively to the topic of kindness, but I've never run across one. What I find interesting is that out of all the topics Greg could have chosen to write about, especially since his field of expertise is broad, he chose kindness. We live in an unkind world, and I'm sad to say, it is populated by many unkind Christians. The Secret Power of Kindness could easily be used as a curriculum for small groups or a sermon series for Pastors."

—Dave Jacobs, author, pastoral coach,
and church consultant

"I've never met a person that would say they don't want to be kind, but through the demands on our lives that push, pull, and pressure us, we can quickly find ourselves in habits that are very different from the abundant life of Jesus. Today, we all need good pushes and godly reminders. Greg has been a chiseling part of my life for a long time, and God has used him to give me these gentle, grace-filled reminders of living a better way. In Greg, I've seen a track record and thread of kindness in every season of his life. I hope this book will be that gentle reminder and that good push in your life like it has been in mine, which allows God to recalibrate you more in the likeness of Jesus."

—Cory Singleton, Church Planting Catalyst, North Ameri-
can Mission Board / Director of GenSend LA

"I wish I had written this book—it's kindness dynamite! I stopped time and again to pick up pieces of wisdom and courage to change as I move forward. Thank you, Greg, for giving us a book that's both a toolkit overflowing with ways to live kindly as well as medicine for soul care —for you and all you are shaping."

—Steve Sjogren, Kindness Outreach Ministries,
KindnessExplosion.Com

"Greg Atkinson is one of my closest friends on this planet. He is truly one of the kindest people I know. While we were in college together, I don't think I ever paid for a meal, especially being the broke brotha' that I was during those times. But, little did I know he was just as broke as me but always gave extravagantly and recklessly out of love and a generous heart. That love was also expressed through many late-night college binges at Little Pappy's, where he would pay for the meals of the homeless and the less fortunate. It was always a sight to see us try to share Jesus with intoxicated patrons at the restaurant. At the end of those nights after our adventures, he would, of course, always leave sweet tips for Ms. Diane, no matter how mean she would be toward us at the drop of a dime, depending on the night. Trust me when I say this book will challenge and motivate you. These words will touch your heart and possibly your wallet in a tremendously kind way toward others if you let it."

—Thomas Rose, Rose Factor Music and Dream Streets North Nashville Director

"Greg Atkinson. When I look up the word, "kindness" in my pictoral dictionary of English words, why is it I see his picture? Knowing Greg personally and professionally for years, it only seems natural for him to be the guy who writes on the Secret Power of Kindness. That's who he is . . . and that is the integrity with which this book is written. As you move through the pages of these ten facets of kindness—ooh, each one is rich in practicality—slow down. Allow the Spirit of God to speak into you with counsel, wisdom, conviction, and guidance. Enjoy the journey through the pages of this book and allow it to transform the pages of your future from the inside out! And buy a copy for your spouse, boss, and kid's teacher. The world needs a lot more kindness!"

—Dr. Matthew Lee Smith, adventurer, ambassador, author and Executive Director of Eagles in Leadership

<<MORE ENDORSEMENTS TO COME—AUTHOR WILL PROVIDE<]>>

THE
SECRET
POWER OF
KINDNESS

GREG ATKINSON

Foreword by Mark Batterson

THE SECRET POWER OF

KINDNESS

10 Keys to Unlocking Your Potential for Good

invite
PRESS

Plano, Texas

THE SECRET POWER OF KINDNESS:
10 KEYS TO UNLOCKING YOUR POTENTIAL FOR GOOD

Copyright 2023 by Greg Atkinson

This book is printed on acid-free, elemental chlorine-free paper.

ISBN 978-1-953495-71-6; epub 978-1-953495-72-3

23 24 25 26 27 28 29 30 31 32—10 9 8 7 6 5 4 3 2 1
MANUFACTURED IN THE UNITED STATES OF AMERICA

To my three kids, Grace, Tommy, and Katie, who are the sweetest and kindest kids I could ask for. I'm so proud to be their dad.
To Jerry Stepp, who not only invested in me and changed the trajectory of my life but is the kindest person I know.
To my father-in-law, George Montagno, who is a kind and gentle soul, and the memory of my wife's cousin, Kris Petterson, who was one in a million, and although she left this world at the young age of twenty-six, she made an impact on innumerable lives. Kris, you lit up a room. May our world see more people live and be like you.
To my wife, Amanda, thanks for your constant love and support.

CONTENTS

FOREWORD

Humankind. What if we thought of it as two words instead of one? Kindness is embedded into our name, but it's all too often absent. In fact, kindness feels like a lost art form. That changes with this book. As Greg Atkinson says, "Kindness is a secret weapon. It disarms people and breaks down their defensive walls." In other words, kindness is our de-escalation technique. There is no defense against genuine kindness.

For many years I've admired Greg Atkinson's work. He's someone who rallies people around kingdom causes. He's someone who empowers other people. He's someone who brings out the best in others. So, it's no surprise that's what this book does.

Along with the nuts and bolts of kindness, Greg goes deeper, into theology and psychology. Why is kindness so powerful? Because it mirrors what God Himself models! Romans 2:4 is a linchpin in my theology: "God's kindness leads you to repentance." When God wants us to change, He shows us kindness. And if that doesn't work? He shows us more kindness! Maybe, just maybe, we should follow suit.

Kindness may seem old-fashioned, but in truth it's omni-relevant. "If you want new ideas," said Ivan Pavlov, "read old books." The same is true of "old virtues" like kindness. Of course, it's more than a virtue. It's a fruit of the Spirit.

I have a theory for everything: *the answer to every prayer is more of the Spirit*. But what about love? Or joy? Or peace? Those are fruits of the Spirit, just like kindness. So, what we really need is more of the Spirit that produces more of that fruit.

As you read this book, I hope and pray it produces a rising tide of kindness. And as Greg so aptly points out, be kind to yourself. We often forget that the Great Commandment is three-dimensional. We know we need to love God and love people. But it's hard to love others if you don't like yourself. The hardest person to forgive is the person who stares back at you in the mirror every day! Be kind to that person, and you'll be kinder to others.

The old axiom is true: people don't care how much you know until they know how much you care. We find ourselves in a cultural moment where people simply want to feel seen, heard, and loved. The good news? A little kindness goes a long way. It's time for this overlooked and underappreciated fruit of the Spirit to get its due.

Ready or not, be kind.

—Mark Batterson, *New York Times* bestselling *author* of The Circle Maker

PREFACE

"The secret power of kindness is the self-awareness to know that you have the power to make or break someone else's day and eventually change the world. Kindness has no hidden agenda or strings attached. Its only purpose is to express love to another soul made in the image of God."

—Greg Atkinson

"Kindness has been defined as loaning someone your strength instead of reminding them of their weakness."

—Brené Brown

"Kind words soothe and quiet and comfort the hearer. They pull him out of his sour, morose, unkind feelings. We have not yet begun to use kind words in such abundance as they ought to be used."

—Blaise Pascal

"Always be a little kinder than necessary."

—James M. Barrie

Kindness: noun; the quality of being friendly, generous, and considerate.

Imagine a world where everyone is kind to one another. Don't we all agree that the world needs more kindness? Not only does the world need more kindness but it would be a better place if we each displayed kindness in our daily lives.

As Christians, we believe that kindness is one of the fruits of the Spirit that flows out of us naturally when we are abiding in Christ.

The more time you spend with Jesus, the kinder you will be. But kindness is also a choice that comes out of a soul at peace with itself, a soul that feels free.

Whereas we would imagine that Christians should be the kindest people on earth, given our faith in Christ's promise and our commitment to his way of life, most of us know that this is not the case. In fact, sometimes it seems that we struggle more than others to show kindness, especially when our most beloved traditions or opinions are at stake.

But why? What prevents us from behaving kindly toward others? Why is it so hard for us to exude the simple acts of kindness that bind all of us closer as fellow human beings?

As humans, Christians too, sometimes our hearts can get locked into places of pain and fear caused by our experiences with the world, misunderstandings about God, or our own unreasonable expectations of ourselves. Once we become enmeshed in misconceptions, anger, pain, or perfectionism, it can become tough to see ourselves kindly, let alone emit kindness to the world. This can be the case even for the most ardent of Christians.

We live in a complicated world. People today face a myriad of problems. Yet, we know that kindness can be the powerful force we need to make positive change in our world, to unlock anger and bitterness, heal divisions, forge relationships, and foster respect. Think about it. Simply choosing to be kind to someone could be the healing balm that he or she needs that day. Have you ever smiled at a waiter or a cashier who looked beyond stressed or simply blue, and then saw them suddenly light up? Kindness is a secret weapon. It disarms people and breaks down their defensive walls. Kindness unlocks kindness. Complimenting people, commending people, affirming people, and thanking people can make all the difference in their day, their attitude, and in their life and yours.

Kindness changes the way we look at people. To cultivate kindness within ourselves not only helps us to be kind to others but gives us a fresher, easier perspective on life, one that is filled with grace, love, and hope. You never know the impact you may have on an individual simply by practicing the power of kindness.

I've seen many wounded, bitter people who have grown so mean, nasty, and hateful that you couldn't help but see the prison walls that they had built up around their lives. Kindness begins to flow when we free ourselves and others from the walls and fences that divide and confine us.

I invite you to read this book like a mirror. In it, I will show you some ways that you can begin to unlock the prison walls surrounding you—those fears and feelings that are keeping you from feeling God's joy within and from expressing that joy in kindness toward others. Ask God to reveal those areas of your life that you need to address, and pray for the courage to do your part in that work of change as you humbly submit your will to His.

As you delve into this book, my prayer for you is that God would open your eyes to all that you can become for yourself and others. Remarkable change can happen when you realize that you're loved just as you are. Let me share with you what I have learned about unlocking the "secret power" of kindness.

INTRODUCTION

"As long as we remain resentful about things we wish had not happened, about relationships that we wish had turned out differently, mistakes we wish we had not made, part of our heart remains isolated, unable to bear fruit in the new life ahead."

—Henri Nouwen

When I was young, I loved fishing. My favorite place to fish was a pond not far from my home, a quiet place filled with life, simplicity, and the sounds of nature—crickets chirping, birds singing, fish splashing, frogs leaping. Here on the banks of the pond, fishing pole in hand, I felt happy. My soul felt at peace and calm. Often, I would spend the entire day at the pond, catching fish, enjoying the wind in my hair, and listening for God's voice. That was the best part. I could hear God speaking to me in that peaceful place, telling me I was loved.

Having had a difficult and traumatic childhood, the pond was my solace; fishing became my healing balm, and prayer became my comfort. I longed daily for the peace I found in fishing. And yet, that pond was not as easy to access each day as I might have wished. Surrounded by a tall, sturdy fence, the area could only be entered into through a single gateway at the edge of the woods. Nearby stood a shed. When the ranger was in the shed, he would kindly come and unlock the series of padlocks on the gate and grant me access. No matter how many times I came, he always let me in.

When he wasn't there however, I faced a dilemma. The fence was too high to climb, too slim to slide through, and I had no way to open the gate—or so I thought. It took a long time, and a lot of failed attempts, for me to realize that I had access to the keys to unlock that gate all by myself all along.

I could enter the shed, which was always left open. Once I stepped in the door, I knew where to find the box with the keys inside. All I needed to do was to find the right keys to unlock the padlocks on the gate. After that, each time I came to the pond, I began to pay more attention when the ranger unlocked the gate. When the ranger wasn't there, I gradually learned how to gain access all by myself—access to the pond, access to peace, access to the freedom and power inside of me.

Although those days of boyhood are now long past, the lessons learned stay with me to this day. My keys to peace and wellness come from learning how to open the gates to the fences that keep me locked into places of unrest, anger, self-criticism, and doubt.

Through years of unlocking my own fences, I have learned to be kind to myself, unlike those who were unkind to me, and to find peace within myself, unlike the tumult I sought to escape. Then I noticed a pattern. The kinder I felt toward myself, the kinder I became to others.

I have long lamented the plight of all those who have suffered traumas similar to what I endured, or who have felt wounded by illness, poverty, anxiety, other people, or even by the church itself, and who have become locked into places of inaccessibility in their hearts and souls.

Sometimes, we can be hindered simply by our inability to see past untrue things we've been taught about God. Sometimes, we may succumb to the false limitations of rigid dogma, traditions, rituals, or rules that have governed our churches and inhibited us from emotional and spiritual growth. Sometimes, we may suffer from the idea that to be a member of a church requires a level of inhuman perfectionism that we continually fail to meet. Or perhaps we are simply our own inner critics, unaccepting of our imperfections, critical of our mistakes, angry with those who disagree with us, and prone to protect and control our turf. All of these become fences that require unlocking if we want to become the kind and loving people we hope to be.

The truth is, with God's help, we hold the keys to unlock the kind of change we want to see in the world as Christians, in ourselves and in others. We have the power within us to be extraordinarily kind, to be the people of God we were meant to be, to demonstrate over-the-top kindness that goes the extra mile, to start a "kindness movement" that spreads and multiples. But first, we must learn to tap into that "secret" place within us where kindness, love, and peace dwell.

In this book, we will learn about the fences that we allow to form around us, we will identify the keys that will unlock our true kindness potential, we will find that true peace and joy that comes with self-acceptance and love, and we will free ourselves to experience and practice the secret power of kindness.

UNLOCKING FORGIVENESS

How to Replace Hostility and Bitterness with
Mercy and Compassion

*"Be kind to one another, tenderhearted, forgiving one another, as God in
Christ forgave you."*

—Ephesians 4:32 (ESV)

"The most profound thing we can offer our children is our own healing."

—Anne Lamott

John Stott quotes the administrator of the largest psychiatric
hospital in London, who said, "If the people here only knew what it
means to forgive, I could dismiss half of them at once." In the same
way, when a news reporter asked Billy Graham, "What do you see as
the biggest obstacle in people's lives," Reverend Graham responded,
"Unforgiveness. I believe that 75 percent of patients in hospitals
would be made whole if they would forgive." Pain in life is inevi-
table. It is also crushing and devastating. I've been on the highest
mountaintops and in the lowest valleys throughout my nearly fifty
years on planet Earth.

My mentor always said, "Every man or woman has a father
wound and a church wound." I have both. I've been deeply hurt,
wounded, neglected, and abused by my earthly father. I've also been

deeply hurt, wounded, betrayed, and lied about by church members where I previously served as a pastor. If that were not enough, I also suffered the trauma of sexual abuse at a daycare when I was just a young child.

In the following pages you will read about the devastating toxicity of wounds and the healing power of forgiveness. It's vital that you address the emotional and spiritual wounds in your life. If you don't, you will become like a soldier wounded on the battlefield whose toxic wounds go un(a)dressed: that soldier is going to become extremely sick. No matter your trauma or hurt—whether it's family of origin wounds, father wounds, church wounds, sexual abuse wounds, or any other of numerous scenarios—if you don't address your wounds, you're going to become bitter, toxic, and emotionally or spiritually ill. In order to begin to access our inner well of kindness, we will need to start by acknowledging the fences we have erected around us that harbor and perpetuate our wounds. Then we need to start unlocking the parts of ourselves that we have refused to access for fear of stoking and poking those wounds.

The first key then that we need to search for in our toolbox is the key that will unlock our ability to forgive. That key for us is shaped like a caduceus symbol, the pharmacological symbol of healing, because for us, forgiveness is an antidote that can restore our souls to wellness.

The secret power of kindness, when released, can solve most of our problems, not only personally but as a nation collectively. Taking the first step to unlock our ability for forgiveness begins to release that personal power.

How can we talk about initiating forgiveness and kindness in a world that is so cruel? How do we forgive when bad—sometimes unbelievably bad—things happen to us? In this chapter, I'm going to share some thoughts on the secret power of kindness and the key role that forgiveness plays in our lives.

How you deal with the trauma and pain in your life—including how you respond to it—will shape your life presently and in the future. The bottom line is that you have a choice—you can become bitter or better. Kindness is the remedy, and forgiveness is the antidote. There's no doubt in my mind that you can live a whole and healthy life, even if it hurts to get there.

WHY FORGIVENESS MATTERS

"Forgiveness doesn't excuse their behavior. Forgiveness prevents their behavior from destroying your heart."

—**Justin and Trisha Davis,** Beyond Ordinary

When I was a young boy, I was molested and sexually assaulted by a man at a Baptist church daycare. I was around five years old, and I blocked it from my mind—at least I thought I did. As I grew in years, I started thinking, since I was so young, that I was simply confused. Maybe I was mistaken about what happened at the daycare. I blocked it all out, and I went on with life. Later, when I started going to a therapist for other issues in my life, the memories started to come back.

Once, I met with a pastor and mentor. He was unlike many pastors that I had ever known. In fact, he has what's called "a prophetic gift." Without me saying anything, he told me what had happened to me as a boy. As he talked, memories flooded into my mind. Vivid memories. Difficult memories. I remembered everything about the abuse and the perpetrator.

As soon as I got back home, I called someone who was at the daycare with me. I said, "Hey, man, I don't know if you remember that daycare we went to when we were young, but I got molested there." My poor friend—I just blurted it out without so much of a thought as to how it sounded or what he would think. But just as I finished my sentence, he responded, "I know, it happened to me too." I started crying. Even though I was only five when the sexual abuse happened, I felt horrible that I couldn't protect my friend from what I knew was soul-destroying pain and trauma.

Survivors of sexual abuse, especially children, experience trauma through feelings of confusion, fear, humiliation, and shame. When people are abused, shame falls on their shoulders; they feel as though they did something wrong. That shame follows them into adulthood and implants itself into their hearts until they can experience healing. Forgiveness allows them that healing. Forgiveness is not a benefit for the perpetrator, but a healing salve for the victim.

While at therapy I learned that shame is not from God. It originates from the enemy of our souls. God convicts us of sin to bring us out of shame, not to put us into it. Shame often fuels addiction and other unruly behavior, because it drives a person further down into a pit of shame.

God will never shame you. That's not God's way of transforming us. Shame is not rooted in love. Shame and love do not coincide.

Shame silences victims of abuse. We don't want to think about it, and we especially don't want to talk about it. A big part of my healing journey consisted of dealing with the shame that I felt. Once I did, that changed my whole trajectory.

Another difficult part of abuse is lack of validation. When sharing about my own sexual abuse with a family member, my family member replied, "No, you're mistaken. That certainly didn't happen. Absolutely not." There's nothing more painful than to go through trauma like that and then not be validated.

I've been asked a few times what happened to the perpetrator of my abuse. I honestly don't know. Since it was kept hidden for so many years, I don't know if he ever faced the music. But no matter where he is (or even if he's not alive anymore), my journey toward healing would need to include forgiving not only my abuser but also my family member, whether or not that person ever chooses to believe my testimony.

Forgiving means letting go of the anger, pain, shame, and guilt that I carry upon my back and no longer allowing my abuser to have a perpetrating and influential role in my emotional and spiritual life. In forgiving, I render him powerless.

"YOU ARE NOT ALONE"—THE GAPING FATHER WOUND

"The major turning points I've seen for a lot of successful people:
1. The day they give their life to Jesus.
2. The day they forgive their dad."

—Ryan Leak, Twitter, June 19, 2022

"You own everything that happened to you. Tell your stories. If people wanted you to write warmly about them, they should have behaved better."

—Anne Lamott, Twitter, April 23, 2012

My father was a very harsh man. Most of my memories of him consist of me receiving verbal and physical abuse. He was constantly yelling at me. Not surprisingly, I never heard him tell me that he loved me.

While my dad was many things, he was also a man who had been deeply hurt in life. Though I don't know a whole lot about his history, what I do know was that his life was difficult right from the beginning. His dad died in the Spanish Civil War, and his mom died giving birth to him.

My dad grew up in an orphanage until he finally got adopted by the Atkinsons, which of course is how I received my last name. The Atkinsons were a rich family who adopted my dad as little more than a charity case. They didn't give him any attention and certainly didn't give him any affection.

When my dad got to middle school, his adoptive parents decided to send him off to military school. The boarding school was full-time, and though some kids went home for holidays and other special events, my dad did not. The Atkinsons paid for his tuition through high school but never brought him home. In fact, once my dad was sent off to military school, he never saw his parents again for the rest of his life. Can you imagine that? Is it any wonder that my dad lived in a constant state of turmoil?

Of course, I didn't know my father's background until much later in life. So growing up with him was unbearable for me in many

5

ways. My dad would ruin every meal we had, whether we were at home or at a restaurant.

At home, the yelling started as soon as I sat down at the table. He would yell at me to sit up straight (thanks to his experience at military school) and get my elbows off the table. My siblings and I would be in tears trying to eat dinner. He would just destroy the whole mood. Going out to eat was not any better. If something got messed up on his order, he would aggressively lean into the waitress, and because he was so mean, she would end up crying—something that made all of us embarrassed.

The first time I ever brought my college girlfriend (a woman whom I ended up marrying) home to meet my parents turned into a nightmare. We went on a drive with my dad to see a lake front property that he was purchasing. I was in the front seat, and my girlfriend was in the back. It didn't take long into the drive when my father started biting my head off, uncontrollably screaming and yelling at me. I was hurt and upset. My girlfriend had just met him. Wouldn't you think he would have put on a good face for company?

I remember looking out the window at the lake with tears in my eyes, feeling both humiliated and embarrassed. I couldn't believe he was talking to me like this in front of my new girlfriend. Meanwhile, my girlfriend was shell-shocked. This behavior was completely contrary to how her dad interacted with everyone. Of course, I got to know her dad while we were dating and then when we married. Her dad is an exceedingly kind, loving, and gentle man.

I would find out later just how livid my girlfriend was that day at my dad. When she became a part of "our family" through marriage, she would come to see just how harsh my dad was toward me.

When I was 12, I found out that I had half-sisters and a half-brother because my dad had been married before—something he kept secret and hidden from my mom. When my dad met my mom, she said she would never marry somebody who had been divorced. So, my dad just kept it a secret. That bit of news was traumatizing to me and rocked my world.

I thought I was my dad's firstborn (the only thing I felt I had going for me). My dad's name is Tom, and I had always wondered why

I wasn't named after him. Well, he already had another son named Tom.

When I met my counselor for the first time and gave her all the information regarding my dad (with a lot more details, I'm afraid), she looked me in the face and said, "You had a very traumatizing childhood."

Later, I would meet my half-brother, Tom, who was terribly angry, having grown up without his dad in his life. He became a Christian and worked through the process of forgiving our dad. Today, Tom and I have a good relationship, and we are always in awe at how God brought us together and worked in both of our lives to bring about much-needed healing through the balm of forgiveness. Recently, at a Boston Red Sox baseball game, Tom told me, "You know, it's funny. I've always wanted a brother."

My dad died of a heart attack on May 27, 1997. He was sixty years old. I was just twenty-one years old. On the day he died, I had been reading my Bible, specifically Psalm 66. I read the verse where it says that God is "a father to the fatherless" and circled it. It caught my interest, as I had never noticed that verse before. Next to the circled verse, I wrote the day's date, 5-27-97, a habit I had gotten into when I noticed something I had never seen before in Scripture. Later that same day, my Uncle Joel called me and told me my dad had just died of a heart attack.

It's been twenty-six years since my dad died. A large part of my healing journey came about by realizing that God is the father I never had. He's a father to the fatherless. This was huge for me. Many people struggle with the concept of God, especially God as their heavenly Father, because they had an imperfect earthly father. Maybe as you're reading this, you can relate to what I'm saying. Perhaps your father is a mean man, harsh, abusive, or mostly absent, and you just can't relate to God as a father figure. I get it. I struggled with the same concept until I realized that God is a father to the fatherless. He's the perfect Father I never had—one that loves me perfectly, brings about healing in my life, and provides great comfort.

For the last twenty-six years I have related to God in a whole new way as a father, something I couldn't do as a boy. I wish I'd seen that verse when I was younger. However, I find it loving and special that God would show me that verse on the actual date of my dad's death. It was as if God was preparing me for the news and saying, "Hey, look at this verse, I'm a father to the fatherless." It was a special embrace from God that nudged me towards my healing journey.

It would take a long time for me to truly forgive my father. But seeing God as my true father helped me to begin to unlock my ability to forgive and to heal that gaping wound inside.

THE DEEP WOUNDS OF CHURCH HURT

"God heals the brokenhearted and bandages their wounds."

—*Psalm 147:3 (CEB)*

One of the reasons I speak often at mental health conferences is because I have bipolar disorder. There's still a huge stigma attached to mental illness—especially bipolar disorder. People think bipolar means crazy, which is not the case at all. In fact, many people with bipolar disorder are intelligent, operate businesses, have families, and hold leadership positions in the community.

My wife, myself, and our kids were living in Missouri in 2011. We loved it, and it easily became our home. I had worked in the community and really wanted to place down roots. I interviewed with a popular multi-campus church in our area. I was extremely excited about the prospect of becoming a campus pastor. During the interview for the job, I was upfront, and told them I had a mood and anxiety disorder. They were not bothered by that news and in fact said, "That's not a problem."

I got the job and started working at one of the campuses almost immediately. I really loved being a campus pastor. Along with our team, we reached out to the community in many ways, and it was a blessing to see the church grow. In fact, in a short amount of time, we tripled our attendance. Our campus also set records for baptisms. We were busting out of the seams. The lead pastor of the church was thrilled with what was going on at my campus. We had built a good relationship, and he would hug me every week and say, "You're doing such an excellent job. You're the man. You're doing great."

I had been with the church for about two and a half years, and I really felt that I should share with the lead pastor about being bipolar. So, when I saw him in the hall one day, I told him that I wanted to tell him something about me. He said, "Man, Greg, you can tell me anything."

I thought to myself, *well, we will see.*

Weeks later, in a meeting, I said, "Remember when you hired me, and I told you that I had a mood and anxiety disorder?"

"Sure, I remember that. It wasn't a big deal," he said.

I looked at him and said, "Well, that mood disorder is actually bipolar—that's what I have."

His whole facial expression changed—he looked angry.

A month later, the lead pastor asked my wife and me to meet with him and the executive pastor. As we sat in the office, my wife and I were stunned when the lead pastor coldly read a letter that said I was being fired because the insurance company could not provide liability coverage for a pastor / counselor with bipolar disorder. It was a shocking proclamation. The lead pastor made it sound as though his hand was forced, that if he didn't let me go, they would lose their liability insurance. This reason ended up not being true.

The *Wall Street Journal* wrote an article on the subject, and when they interviewed the church's insurer, GuideOne Insurance, they denied that they ever said that or participated in the matter.[1] I knew the lead pastor had lied. He had operated out of his own prejudices, bias, and views of bipolar.

I chose to take the high road. I decided to resign to keep the peace and unity in the church and agreed to write a letter (that church leadership would have to approve) that would be read to the congregation. I asked if I could meet with the lead pastor once again before my final day at the church. When I met with him in his office, another pastor was there as well. The lead pastor was anxious

---

1. Ian Lovett, January 20, 2020, *Wall Street Journal*, https://www.wsj.com/articles/its-like-i-got-kicked-out-of-my-family-churches-struggle-with-mental-health-in-the-ranks-11579547221.

and asked me three times in the meeting, "Are you going to sue us?" He had reason to be anxious. The American Disabilities Act (ADA) states that it's illegal to fire somebody or not hire somebody due to mental health reasons. The lead pastor asked me yet again, "Are you going to sue us?" I politely said, "No, I'm not going to sue you."

On my last day of church, the lead pastor came to our campus. After I read my resignation letter, I sat down up front, so the lead pastor could deliver the sermon. But before he started to preach, he told the congregation that after the service they could come down front to hug me and say goodbye.

The line of people was long. Besides the pleasant words and hugs, I also got whispers in my ear—"I have depression and have never told anyone. Thank you for your courage," "I have anxiety. Thank you for speaking up," "I have bipolar too. Thank you for being so brave." The whispers kept coming, one after another, after another.

Twenty-five percent of people sitting in church today have mental health issues. After the coronavirus pandemic, this percentage rose even higher.

Thanks to the *Wall Street Journal* article, much needed attention was placed on how we deal with mental illness as a society—not only in our country but in our churches as well. I was encouraged by the many calls and emails I received from Christian leaders around the nation.

Working in ministry is a beautiful calling, but it can also be disappointing when one is faced with situations in which Christians don't behave like Christ. I have worked at three mega churches and have had the experience of feeling chewed up and eventually spit out when not needed anymore. Sadly, when people experience church hurt—whether they work in ministry or attend a church where they have had a traumatic experience—they often walk away from their faith or become angry with God.

But church leaders are just people—flawed, sinful humans, just like the rest of us. Shouldn't they be a good example and take accountability for their actions? Yes, of course. I was disappointed in some of the leaders I worked for and was hurt by this as well. But in order to begin to forgive, we need first to see our leaders and peers as fellow human beings with their own sins and foibles.

In our culture we tend to idolize people. We put them up on a pedestal until they come crashing down. Then we walk away from what they represented. We idolize pastors—especially mega-church pastors—and treat them like rock stars. Then the moment they do something wrong, we crash. Our idol is broken, and we walk away from God, as if we are surprised that Christians are, well, human.

When I say this, I'm not minimizing the wounds I have from church hurt. In our culture, in which we see sex abuse cases raging in churches and even in the higher ranks of denominations, it is critical that churches remain accountable and that survivors of abuse or church hurt are heard and protected. But for those who know Christ, we need to realize that we are following Christ, not the pastor or the leader who did wrong.

Through the hurts I experienced by leaders in church, I found an ever-increasing faith in God. God was always my comforter and my defender, and God would be my healer as well.

FORGIVING MEANS LETTING GO OF WHAT "SHOULD" HAVE BEEN

Forgiving is always a process. When I was let go (resigned) from the church in Missouri, my plans came crashing down. I had planned to be at the church and in that community for the long haul. I loved southwest Missouri, the church, and the community. I wanted my kids to graduate from the local high school, Carthage. My ministry career was flourishing, and I was receiving invitations to talk at conferences around the nation. But when my job was terminated, so was the vision and plans of what I had expected to be a life-long endeavor in that church and in that community.

All my heroes in ministry have been at their churches for twenty years or more. They committed to a particular church, a particular community, and that area of service. I wanted that for myself. I didn't want to jump around from church to church, or town to town. I wanted to stay somewhere for decades. However, that would not be my story. I not only had to forgive the pastor who lied in Missouri but also other pastors or leaders who promised me the world but fell short on delivering. I had to grieve that I wouldn't have a several-decades-long ministry at this particular church.

My family and I ended up moving back to the Southeast, specifically to South Carolina. That's where my kids ended up graduating high school. No, it wasn't my vision to be there, but I would find out along the way that my story really was God's story. And God had a plan.

While still in Missouri (though no longer working at the church), I did what had become a custom for me—I flew to Spartanburg, South Carolina, to speak at a worship conference. This was something I did yearly. It was only ten minutes from where I grew up and where my mom, sister, and aunt still lived. On a break from the conference, I met my mom and aunt for lunch. They had just picked up Mark Batterson's book, *Draw the Circle: 40-Day Devotional.* It was based on his *New York Times* best seller, *Circle Maker.* They couldn't stop talking about the devotional book. I've known Mark for years. He's a longtime friend. So when I got back to the conference, I bought a copy of Mark's book.

While in the hotel room, I started reading it. The very first devotional day I read made me think about my grief over "what could have been" my life in Missouri. But then something happened. I realized that my life in Missouri was nothing like what I had planned and hoped it to be. I was in the middle of the country, far from family, humiliated and embarrassed that I lost my job. I was the guy going to the grocery store who everybody knew used to be the pastor at the big church in town, the pastor with mental illness. It was as though a light turned on in my brain and in my heart. I prayed, "God, bring me home." I decided to move my family back to South Carolina— my home state—and to be there for my mom as she started to age.

By the time I read day 40 in Mark Batterson's devotional, Transformation Church in South Carolina called and said, "You got the job. You're moving here." They paid for my move from Missouri to the Carolinas.

I'm amazed by how God brings good things out of bad stuff that happens in our lives. He used my horrible circumstances, and even Mark Batterson's book, to get me back home, all expenses paid.

Now, I'd like to be able to say that I stayed for decades at Transformation Church, but that job only lasted a year, because they shut down my campus. Yes, I went through hurt and pain again, but it wasn't as severe. Why? I was thankful to be home—to be where I wanted to be, and though short, my job with Transformation accomplished that prayer.

There was also something else that made the situation fine. After being laid off in South Carolina, I wrote a devotional titled *Take Courage: Winning the War on Fear*, on mental health for the YouVersion Bible App.[2] Well over a hundred thousand people around the world have read that devotional. People have been helped. Because of the loss of jobs in my life, I ended up working for myself and have been grateful for all of the doors that God has opened for me to serve in a way that helps others both inside and outside of the church.

EXPERIENCING HEALING THROUGH FORGIVENESS

"You are not responsible for how other people have hurt you. But . . . you are 100 percent responsible for how long you let their hurt dominate your life."

—*Perry Noble*

We're not going to be kind people if we don't learn to forgive those who have hurt us. I believe everyone wants to find healing and wholeness and not live in a prison of bitterness, anger, and depression. Problematically, though, I also believe that many people either don't know how to find wholeness or they don't want to face the trauma that they have experienced in their life. Sometimes living in denial seems safer than facing those horrible truths. However, as someone who has experienced trauma and denial, I can say that the path toward healing, though often difficult, is worth the journey.

---

2. Greg Atkinson, The Bible App, "Take Courage: Winning the War on Fear," accessed Mar. 29, 2023, https://www.bible.com/reading-plans/3121-take-courage.

Nothing compares to living life free from the emotional and physical effects of trauma and woundedness. Living in freedom—freedom from bitterness, hate, and mental anguish—enables you to love and forgive people, to be compassionate and empathetic, and truly to be kind to all of the people you meet.

Are you looking for wholeness? Are you tired of living in a prison of bitterness and hate? It's time to get help and healing by unlocking your ability to forgive.

I'm a big proponent of seeking professional help through counseling and therapy to assist one on their journey toward healing and wholeness. I've been to individual therapy, couples therapy, and group therapy. I've been in therapy programs that are on-site, like Onsite in Tennessee—they do nine days of therapy that equals nine months of therapy. I have a ton of friends who have done the on-site program. This type of program addresses your family of origin, trauma, woundedness, sexual abuse, childhood trauma, and more. I've invested both money and hours into therapy, because I didn't want what happened to me when I was younger to rule and dominate my life. I wanted to be whole.

If you don't forgive those who hurt you, you will never find healing. If you never find healing for the trauma and the hurts that you have faced, you will live in bondage—a prison of bitterness, anger, hate, and hardness. And this will affect not only your life but those around you as well. Without healing, you won't move forward in life. You will be stuck in a constant childhood state of trauma.

Forgiveness is a process. But the more you are able to forgive, the more you will free yourself to experience kindness, and to give it to others too.

HURT PEOPLE HURT PEOPLE—AND THEY ARE MISERABLE TOO

It's an old saying that has become a cliché, but it's also a golden nugget of truth: "Hurt people hurt people." If you have not been able to forgive and move on from what happened to you as a child (or an adult), you're going to be a mean, grumpy, inconsiderate, and bitter person. You're not going to be fun to be around. You're not going to be loving. You're just going to be a jerk to people.

Hurt people hurt people. Wounded people wound people. But rescued people rescue people.

I've been blessed with the opportunity to help others on their healing journeys. It's wonderful to help others and be an advocate for those who have been traumatized, abused, and treated poorly in life.

Everyone's healing journey is unique. There's no set pattern of time when it comes to finding wholeness. It could take years, decades, or even happen in an instant. Even though I'm a proponent of therapy, I believe that it is God who does the healing. The power of God can heal any wounded heart. He can take a hard heart and make it soft again, and He can transform a bitter heart into one that forgives. God can do that in an instant via prayer, or He can do it over time. The biggest step you will ever take toward healing is learning to forgive.

When I got wounded by my church, I forgave my boss—I took him to lunch and said, "I love you and I forgive you," and then I hugged him. Forgiveness releases you from seeking revenge. Forgiveness recognizes that every human being is flawed and damaged in some way. Forgiveness allows you to unload the emotional baggage that keeps you from entering into a place of joy, peace, comfort, and love.

When you forgive your dad, when you forgive that person who abused you, or when you forgive the source of your trauma, your heart and mind will start to change. When you work through the process of healing, when you pray, when you seek counseling and therapy, you can find wholeness and live a joyful, peaceful, fruitful life that responds naturally to people with kindness. And if there's something all of us need in our lives, it is more kindness.

None of this is easy, but if you're up for it, I invite you to continue on in this book as we keep unlocking keys to our inner power of kindness. You can do it. I believe in you. But most of all, I believe in the goodness of God.

Key Two

UNLOCKING GENEROSITY

How to Make Every Season a Season of Gratitude and
Selfless Giving

"A generous person will prosper; whoever refreshes others will be refreshed"
—Proverbs 11:25 (NIV)

"For the past three days, Fred Barley had been sleeping in a tent on the campus of Gordon University in Georgia. Hungry and homeless, he had been unsuccessful in finding work, when he needed to survive. As two police officers approached Fred, they questioned him why he was sleeping on campus. And what they then learned affected them profoundly. Fred had traveled six hours on a bicycle in 100-degree weather so that he could attend his second year in college. With no support, his plan was to camp until school began a few weeks later. And during that time, Fred had hoped to find work.

"Touched by this 19-year old's desire to succeed, the two officers spent their own money for a motel room for Fred. Word then traveled throughout the community about Fred's situation and their acts of generosity. The owner of the motel allowed Fred to stay there until school reopened. A local pizzeria gave Fred a job as a dishwasher. And most importantly, the community started a GoFundMe donation page for Fred that raised over $180,000.

"What began as acts of generosity by two officers, blossomed into an entire community giving back. Today, the community of Conyers continues to show a spirit of generosity through several charity events to help low-income families."

—Reader's Digest

Has someone's generosity touched you? Were you flat broke, not knowing how you could buy groceries or put gas in your car to get to work? Then, out of nowhere, someone at church gave you some money to bless you. Or you went to your mailbox to get your mail, and you opened an envelope that mysteriously contained a check from a friend with a kind note? That is the blessing of generosity.

Maybe, instead of money, you have been touched by someone generously giving of his or her time. Maybe you've been isolated during the Covid-19 pandemic and have had no means to get out of the house to get what you need, but generous neighbors or friends have taken it upon themselves to grocery shop for you and deliver the food to your door during the entire time you have been sick.

The second key to unleashing extraordinary kindness involves unlocking generosity in your life. This key's symbol are hands interlocked in the shape of a heart. Take it from your toolbox. You will need it to take your next step in opening up the fences in your life that represent self-centeredness, competitiveness, fear of lack, and lack of connection with others.

It is obvious that we all love to be on the receiving end of generosity, but do we also live a life of generously giving to others? In this chapter we will explore how to be generous—not cheap—with finances, time, and hospitality. You will learn that gratitude and being a good steward of your finances unleashes your ability to be generous, which in turn increases and releases your potential power for kindness. I especially want you to understand God's economy—that when you practice generosity, God multiplies your efforts and your money in ways you can't comprehend. When you become a giver, you will grasp and celebrate the principle, "It's better to give than receive."

THE HEALING BALM OF GENEROSITY

Generosity takes on many personas—gifting your money, giving your time, and showering others with lavish grace, to name a few. But in all ways, unlocking your generosity serves as a healing balm in the lives you touch. It's a kindness that keeps on giving. In our society today, everyone needs a touch of generosity.

I went to my favorite Mexican restaurant today. I love the place, and it was the first outing I took when things started opening again after the isolation of the pandemic. The owner came up to me at my table to greet me, and my waitress was ready to take my order. I've always been a good tipper. I don't say that to boast. Tipping is just a wonderfully important part of my life. I have vivid memories of my dad making waiters and waitresses cry. So, I'm particularly generous to wait staff at restaurants, coffee houses, and other such places. If you're financially able, I encourage you to be a generous tip-giver. Wait staff work hard and are on their feet all day. They make extraordinarily little by way of wages, so tips make a significant difference in their ability to make a living.

But it's not just about giving a good tip when it comes to extending generosity. It's about taking the time to know your waiter, waitress, or barista's name. It's also about showing a generous amount of grace when they get your order wrong, when they are having a difficult day, or when your order is taking a particularly long time to arrive. When you unlock generosity in this way, your kindness shows through. Instead of looking grouchy, perhaps you smile and tell them, "No worries," when your order is late or just not right. Showing patience, kindness, a smile, or calling them by their names goes a long way to encourage and brighten their day.

Due to Covid-19 and the economy, most restaurants, retail, and other service-oriented places are understaffed. The other day my wife needed to have some work done on our car, so I called our local garage, Palmetto Tire and Service, and was told that they only had two men working this week. They asked if I could bring the car in the following week when they would have three technicians working.

Most of the coffee houses too, like Starbucks, were closing far earlier than their normal closing times due to being understaffed. Instead of letting these circumstances irritate us, how about showing generosity through kindness, patience, and if able, bigger tips? Not only will it go a long way to encourage an already overworked and understaffed workforce but it will also go a long way in making your day one of joy and peace instead of anger and frustration.

LIVING OPENHANDEDLY INSTEAD OF WITH A CLOSED FIST

I learned years ago that if you hold everything you have in open hands to God, He will use your resources to help others and refill your hands, often to overflowing. But if you hold tightly to your possessions, your money, and everything you "own"—not allowing God access—He won't bless your life. The reality is that God owns everything you have, not you. So, bearing all of this in mind, I encourage you to open your hand and use your resources to help others: charities, organizations, and churches.

I just wrote a donation to a nonprofit that I read about and that really touched my heart. They help families of somebody that has suicidal ideation, has attempted suicide, or has committed suicide. They give what they call "life boxes" to families to help them through an exceedingly tough time in their lives. Like most nonprofits, this organization needed financial help as well as firsthand help for their mission. They were going to Uvalde, Texas, which is where a school shooting took place in May 2022. They were going to minister to parents, families, and the community. They did the same thing in Parkland, Florida, after the school shooting there in February 2018. Sadly, research has shown that after school shootings there tends to be a rise in suicides. Parents find it hard to cope and need help.

I received a nice card in the mail from the director thanking me for the donation but also sharing that she was at a loss for words. They were in real need and had been praying for help so they could get to Uvalde and help families. I didn't know that fact when I sent the donation. But that is how God works. When we open our hand to God, He uses our resources and prompts us when there is a need that we may not otherwise even know about.

YOU DON'T HAVE TO BE WEALTHY TO GIVE GENEROUSLY

Mother Teresa lived with the impoverished and the maimed. And even though she did not have wealth, she was one of the most generous people I know. She gave all she had to help others. Mother Teresa not only gave her time and what little resources she had, but she gave her life to those in need. Even with all that this dear woman did to help others, she humbly said, "Not all of us can do great things. But we can do small things with great love."

The life of Mother Teresa reminds me of the biblical story of the "widow's mite":

> And he sat down opposite the treasury and watched the people putting money into the offering box. Many rich people put in large sums. And a poor widow came and put in two small copper coins, which make a penny. And he called his disciples to him and said to them, "Truly, I say to you, this poor widow has put in more than all those who are contributing to the offering box. For they all contributed out of their abundance, but she out of her poverty has put in everything she had, all she had to live on."[3]

Most pastors and people who work in ministry don't make a lot of money. When I pastored in Missouri, we lived on a strict budget and were frugal. And yet, our family and a single woman at church who worked as a cafeteria lunch lady gave more than the two wealthiest people in our church. In fact, that dear lunch lady—just like the widow's mite—gave everything she had.

I often find that those who are the most generous are those with the least. They give their all. They share whatever they have in their cupboards, even if it's little.

Being a Good Steward of All That God Has Given You

---

3. Mark 12:41-44 (ESV).

Everything we have—our money in the bank, the home, and the "material possessions"—has been given to us by God. You might think, "Wait a minute. I've worked hard to earn all that I have." I'm sure you have worked hard, but the reality is that God gave you that talent or gift to do the job that you do. In fact, He gave you that job. And just as it was given to you, it can also be taken away at any moment.

We don't know what the future holds. Any one of us could lose our job tomorrow. I've been laid off numerous times. I know what it's like not only to lose a job but lose everything I have. The truth is, we are merely stewards of the money that God gives us. To be a good steward means that we need to manage our money in a way that glorifies God.

To be a good steward, we need to give prominence to giving rather than hoarding all our money for ourselves. God has given us the resources to live and to share. I have seen some millionaires, and even billionaires, live as misers. While I have seen others, like Bill Gates, be a generous philanthropist, giving away billions of dollars repeatedly to charities and common good organizations. Elon Musk doesn't give to charities even though he is the richest man in the world. Yet when Jeff Bezos, the head of Amazon, got a divorce, and the headlines talked about his wife getting billions in the settlement, what really became "news" was the fact that his now ex-wife, MacKenzie Scott, gave a significant percentage of her settlement to charities.

Whether you make $30,000 a year, $300,000 a year, or even $3,000,000 a year, you can be a good steward of what you've been given.

Years ago, Andy Stanley at North Point Church gave a message where he taught families how to manage their money. He had three jars on the stage. The biggest jar represented living on 80% of what you earn. The second smaller jar represented giving 10% of what you earn. And the last jar represented saving 10% of what you earn. This 80-10-10 money management can be done on any amount of income earned. It's a good formula for helping you to be a good steward of the finances that God has entrusted to you.

I taught this same strategy to my kids when they were young, and it paid off. Today, my adult children are good stewards of their finances and generous when it comes to giving.

YOU CAN'T OUT GIVE GOD—BUT YOU CAN GIVE YOUR STUFF AWAY TO HELP OTHERS

Stephen Olford, in his book, *The Grace of Giving: A Biblical Study of Christian Stewardship*, wrote, "One of the fundamental lessons for Christians is that we cannot outgive God. He is no man's debtor." Henry Parsons Crowell, builder of the great Quaker Oats cereal enterprise, when asked for his average rate of giving, said, "For over forty years I have given sixty to seventy percent of my income to God. But I have never gotten ahead of Him! He has always been ahead of me!"[4]

As a Christian, my motivation to have a generous attitude comes from the ultimate gift giver—God. Jesus doesn't give to us so we can horde it, but so we can bless others. Let's face it, as Americans, we are blessed in many ways with material possessions. For most of us, we can safely admit that we have a whole lot of "stuff." Even the poorest among us would be considered rich by the standards of many countries in the world.

Have you ever looked around your home and asked yourself, "Do I really need so many of these items?" I think most of us could easily give away items in our homes to those who are without and in need.

During our marriage, my wife and I have had several different cars. At some point in our journey, we realized that instead of selling our old car or using it as a trade-in for another vehicle, we could give it to someone who needed a car. One such time was when we

---

4. Henry Parsons Crowell, as quoted by Stephen F. Olford in his book, *The Grace of Giving: A Biblical Study of Christian Stewardship* (Grand Rapids, MI: Kregel, 2000).

gave our older Honda Pilot to a single mom with five kids. Dee was a woman of faith whose husband abandoned her and their kids, even taking the family's only car when he departed. So here was a single mom of five kids, left in the lurch and without any transportation.

My wife and I wanted to surprise Dee with the gift of a car (this was the fourth car I had given away to someone in need). We took our Honda Pilot to a car detailer who got it looking like it was brand new. Before driving it over to her apartment, we asked Dee's friends at church to meet us there to surprise her. We drove the newly detailed Honda to Dee's apartment and parked it right in front of her building. The women from her church small group gathered around the car, and when Dee walked outside, we surprised her! We prayed with Dee and then gave her the keys to the car. Instantly, this single mom had all five of her kids pile into the Honda. With tears streaming down her face, and a heart filled with gratitude, Dee was overwhelmed by God's provision.

We've since given away a fifth car. When you unlock generosity, you not only find it is more blessed to give than to receive but that God will use your life to bring about His care and provision for those you help.

HOSPITALITY AND GENEROSITY ARE TWO SIDES OF THE SAME COIN

"Hospitality means primarily the creation of free space where the stranger can enter and become a friend instead of an enemy. Hospitality is not to change people, but to offer them space where change can take place. It is not to bring men and women over to our side but to offer freedom not disturbed by dividing lines."

—Henri Nouwen, Reaching Out

Hospitality is a lost art in American society. Yet, inviting people into your home to share a meal or to stay awhile is one of the most significant ways to break down barriers, love your neighbor, and turn strangers into friends. In a culture with so much isolation, division, and, sadly, hatred, there is no better way to extend a generous hand than to invite people into your home for dinner and conversation.

My church in South Carolina did a series called "Safe"—are we a safe place? The series was an idea I had and passed on to the pastor of our church. Much like the quote by Henri Nouwen, we were stirred to open our home to those in need of a safe space. We had two recovering alcoholics, one male, and one female, live with us at separate times for about three to four months each. They both were on the road to sobriety. The woman who lived with us for quite a while started her journey toward sobriety on day 1. Each day, as suggested in her Celebrate Recovery class, she would write on her hand, with a pen, each day's number that she had been sober. My wife and I encouraged her on each day of her journey. She got up to day 21 and broke her sobriety by drinking. The very next day, I told her to start over and write day 1 on her hand that night.

When she went all the way up to 365, a year of living sober, we promised that we would take her out to eat wherever she wanted to go. She wanted to go to Chick-fil-A. So, we went out and had a celebration party with our family and all her friends. To this day, she is doing well, and we are blessed to be a part of her healing journey.

While I was a pastor, we had a man stay with us who lost his wife to divorce due to his alcoholism. He wanted to get sober and repair the damage he had done to his family. So, when we brought him into our home, it was a safe space for him to find freedom from alcoholism. As this man walked his healing journey toward recovery, his wife and son started to visit him and encourage him as well. As time went on, his family wanted to reunite. He stayed with us until he was ready to get remarried and move back in with his family. I had the honor of remarrying this couple and still have pictures from their wedding where their son held a sign that said, "Just Re-Married." This wonderful couple and family are still together today. In fact, I recently saw they had just gotten back from a trip to France. Both the husband and wife had gotten their master's degrees and were working on their doctorates.

You may be reading this and wondering if having people in our home with substance abuse was difficult for our children. I do want to be clear that to open your home to someone in need, you need to make sure that everybody in your family is on board. In our family's experience, I can't overemphasize enough how it spoke volumes to our kids. They have witnessed throughout their years of growing up mom and dad helping people, having them in our home, and having them at our dinner table. Now that our kids are adults, they have the same generous spirit of hospitality.

I've hosted all kinds of people at my house—some who lived with us while they got back on their feet and others whom we enjoyed sharing our dinner table with, whether they were strangers, colleagues, neighbors, friends, or students.

I've seen many people in need. Lately, my wife and I have been thinking about single women in a pregnancy crisis who need support, and there is no better way to tend to their care than to give them a safe space to stay while they navigate their journey as single moms.

Maybe the thought of bringing "strangers" into your home to live is something that you struggle with. It may not be something that you feel comfortable doing. I understand that. But there is something that you can do to show hospitality. Invite people over to share a meal and conversation. That colleague at your workplace, that neighbor who lives next door and is all alone, that person who thinks or believes differently than you—invite him or her over for a meal. There is nothing more friendly and personal than opening your home to others. It breaks down walls and turns strangers (or even enemies) into friends.

At the time I am writing this chapter, we just finished hosting a recovering addict and alcoholic for six months. For half a year, we've been pouring into this man daily, trying to help him get back on his feet. Currently, he has a new full-time job that pays him well, and he has transitioned out of our home. After him, another man who needed a place to stay for two months, stayed with us.

In his book, *Crazy Busy*, Kevin DeYoung writes, "Opening our home to others is a wonderful gift and a neglected discipline in the church. But we easily forget the whole point of hospitality. Think of it this way: Good hospital-ity is making your home a hospital. The idea is that friends and family and wounded and weary people come to your home and leave helped and refreshed!"[5]

BECOMING THE HANDS AND FEET OF JESUS

"Then the King will say to those on his right, 'Come, you who are blessed by my Father, inherit the kingdom prepared for you from the foundation of the world. For I was hungry, and you gave me food, I was thirsty, and you gave me drink, I was a stranger and you welcomed me, I was naked, and you clothed me, I was sick, and you visited me, I was in prison, and you came to me.' Then the righteous will answer him, saying, 'Lord, when did we see you hungry and feed you, or thirsty and give you drink? And when did we see you a stranger and welcome you, or naked and clothe you? And when did we see you sick or in prison and visit you?' And the King will answer them, 'Truly, I say to you, as you did it to one of the least of these my brothers, you did it to me.'"

—Matthew 25:34-40 (ESV)

In the Scripture passage above, Jesus tells His followers that when they care for and serve others, they are caring for and serving God. Think about that for a minute. When you choose to be generous with your time, your possessions, your money, and even your home, by helping and caring for others, Jesus says that you're doing these things for Him.

I've always loved this verse because it shows just how much God values, loves, and cares for people—especially those who are in need, in prison, sick, marginalized, and oppressed. When you see that waiter or waitress at the restaurant, treat him or her as you would treat Jesus. When you see that single mom, a neighbor in distress,

---

5. Kevin DeYoung, *Crazy Busy: A (Mercifully) Short Book about a (Really) Big Problem* (Wheaton, IL: Crossway, 2013).

a prisoner, a homeless person, a person struggling with substance abuse, an orphan, someone without a friend, and more . . . God wants you to see His face in all of them. When Jesus was on this earth, He said the "Son of Man did not come to be served, but to serve, and give his life as a ransom for many."

A term that is often used in church circles to describe our role in serving others is "being the hands and feet of Jesus." It's the very embodiment of the gospel. We live it out by loving and serving others with open hands, open wallets, open homes, and open hearts.

BE THE CHURCH

The body of Christ has an opportunity to be the hands and feet of Jesus and change our communities, our states, our nation, and our world. I always say that we need to BE the church, not just go to church. The "church" is people, not a building.

My parent's generation grew up thinking that church was just a building—a place where we go on Sunday and check the box, and then go home and live a separate life Monday through Saturday. We need to be a part of the church body and interact in our community, making a difference in the lives of people right where we live.

Too often we look at the problems in the world and think that we are unable to make any substantial difference. We may not be able to help everyone, but we can certainly help someone. This reminds me of the starfish analogy. A child is walking along the beach and picks up a starfish and throws it into the ocean. An adult approaches and says, "Hey, what are you doing?" The child looks up and says, "I'm helping the starfish!" The adult points to all the other starfish down the beach and says, "Look, you haven't even made a dent! Do you think it really matters?" The child looks at the adult and replies, "It mattered to the one I just threw back into the water." Mother Teresa said, "I alone cannot change the world, but I can cast a stone across the waters to create many ripples."

If each one of us, in each of our own communities, cares about and serves those that come our way, we can create many ripples that reverberate around the globe and make this world a much better place. Unlocking our ability to be generous takes intentionality. We need to sometimes overcome our inhibitions, self-focus, and worry about ourselves and focus our eyes on others. In doing so, we can begin to feel our hearts warm and fill with the joy of giving.

Key Three

UNLOCKING COMPOSURE

Redirect Your Anxiety, Let Go of the Need to Control,
and Stay Calm Under Pressure

*"But if we hope for what we do not see, we wait eagerly for it with patience
and composure."*

—*Romans 8:25 (AMP)*

I'd like to share with you two diametrically opposed coaching styles of two well-known basketball coaches. The first coach is Bobby Knight. As Indiana's basketball coach, he was not known for his equanimity. In one game, he thought that a referee had given his team a bad call. Storming around the gym, he swore at the referee, which caused him to be kicked out of the game and subsequently fined $10,000. Later, at a press conference, coach Knight ranted and raved, never once changing his stance on the referee's call, which of course wasn't changed to suit his anger. My guess is that many people remember coach Knight as a winner. But I remember him as someone who lacked composure. None of his wins matter, in my opinion.

The second coach is John Wooden. As UCLA's basketball coach, he was known as a devout man of faith. Once, his team experienced UCLA's longest winning streak. However, in the final seconds of a game with the University of Houston, the streak of eighty-eight wins came to an end, partly due to a controversial call a referee made that went against his team. After the loss, coach Wooden was asked, "Do you think that call lost the game for you and ended your winning streak?" Coach Wooden smiled. "You never know about those things. There probably was a call or two that went our way. I just want to congratulate Houston's coach and the Houston players for an excellent game." My guess is that many people remember coach Wooden as both a winner *and* a man of true composure.

I share these two stories because, as followers of Jesus, when we feel that we've been slighted by society, how we respond is important. Will we lose our patience, or will we keep our composure?

What causes us to lose our composure? Maybe we need to define what composure is first. Composure means a calmness in our mind, our words, and our actions. In other words, it's a person's ability to self-regulate his or her emotions and reactions—especially in adverse circumstances or situations.

Composure can be seen as one of the attributes of the "fruits of the Spirit." As believers in Christ, we are to be ruled by His spirit, which produces characteristics that we would see in Jesus. The Bible tells us that the fruits of the spirit are love, joy, peace, patience, kindness, goodness, faithfulness, gentleness, and self-control.[6]

No wonder composure is one of the keys to kindness. Think about it for a minute. When looking at the comparison of coach Bobby Knight and coach John Wooden, it's obvious which one exuded kindness, patience, and peace amid stressful situations, right? The reality, for any one of us, is that without having composure, we will have a short fuse, a lack of patience, and fly off the handle when we are anxious, stressed, angry, or fearful, reacting in ways that are far from being kind.

In order to unlock our inner composure, we need yet another key from our toolbox. I like to think of this key as bearing the symbol of a leaf—our symbol of calm, the same calm I felt in my daily fishing expeditions. Anger, anxiety, impatience, and stress can cause us to react in ways that ramp up our heart rate and fire up our temper. As a reactionary mechanism, this part of our defense system is

6. Galatians 5:22-23.

like an electric fence that sends sparks at anyone who dares to draw near.

Often anger and anxiety come from expecting too much from ourselves, of setting ourselves up for perfectionistic goals or unrealistic bars. If we live our lives measuring ourselves against others or trying to control our outcomes, we will live constantly in a state of high anxiety.

In this chapter, I want you to learn the paradox that "letting go is more freeing than having the illusion of control." You can overcome fear, anxiety, and the need to control others by living a life of faith and trust in God. Jesus said, "If you try to hang on to your life, you will lose it. But if you give up your life for my sake, you will save it."[7] Surrender brings peace, and the release of control stops the stress of trying to play God. The need to control the circumstances in our lives, or control others, induces more and more anxiety and stress. The only kind of "control" that should earmark our lives is that of self-regulation—self-control of the emotions, thoughts, and behaviors that run contrary to Christ. Even in this, it is God's Spirit that gives us the power and strength to be someone of composure. The more we embrace a big and healthy view of God—one that strengthens our faith in Him—the more peace we will have in the storms and chaos of life.

Dwight L. Moody said, "A great many people are trying to make peace, but that has already been done. God has not left it for us to do; all we have to do is enter into it."[8]

REDIRECT YOUR ANXIETY

"Anxiety weighs down the heart, but a kind word cheers it up."

—**Proverbs 12:25 (NIV)**

Before we talk about the difficulties concerning anxiety, I want to be clear that there is a difference between "clinical anxiety disorders" and the type of anxiety that human beings can face on any

---

7. Matthew 16:25 NLT.
8. The D. L. Moody Center, "The Quotable Mooday," accessed Mar. 23, 2023, https://moodycenter.org/the-quotable-moody-d-l-moody-quotes/.

given day. Anyone who is familiar with me, my ministry, and my writing, knows that I have an anxiety disorder and take medication accordingly. In fact, the subject of anxiety and our mental health is something I speak on frequently. Whether you struggle with an anxiety disorder or the day-to-day anxiety that often afflicts most human beings, God wants us to live in a place of faith and peace.

Though I take medication that has helped in innumerable ways, I still can face anxious thoughts. If we give in to the fear and worry that drives our anxiety, we certainly can lose our composure. So, what do we do when it comes to anxiety? Are there practical things we can do to redirect our anxious thoughts and emotions? Yes, there are. Two things I recommend in order for us to unlock our power of composure are focusing on God and remembering self-care. We need to take our focus off of our worries and ourselves and unhook our unreasonable expectations from our brows. Unlocking our composure will help us to learn to be kind to ourselves, as well as to others. When we feel calm, we feel kind.

FOCUS ON GOD

When feeling anxious, first, we need to redirect our minds to focus on God. There are many ways to do this. When I read scripture, it gets my mind off of my fear and worry and back onto God's faithfulness and goodness. It's true what Proverbs says about a "good word cheering us up." That's why redirecting our thinking on the truth of God's promises and faithfulness to care for us helps us to see that our fears and worries are often exaggerated or even unfounded. Even when in a situation that is difficult or poses a substantial cause of fear or worry, when we redirect that thought to the power, faithfulness, and love that God has for us (and in us) it changes our perspective from one of hopelessness to one of peace and hope. Remember, nothing is impossible with God.

Communicating with God through prayer is a vital way for us to redirect anxious thoughts. God knows what we are thinking—He knows what is causing our anxiety, our fear, and our worry. By giving Him our anxious thoughts—surrendering them to Him to carry— we can release the burden of our situation to the God who loves us and has a good plan for us. Your faith grows the more time you spend in prayer and in Bible reading.

Meditation and journaling have been an immense help and source of comfort to me. It's a bit different than praying or even reading biblical passages alone. In meditation, I'm focused on being present with God. It's intentional. It's not just me speaking to God but a two-way conversation in which I also *listen* to God. He might bring a Scripture to my mind, and as I read it, I start to write down in my journal what the Lord is telling me through His Word. I also include music in my meditation. When we worship God, it changes our hearts and minds. Often when I am meditating in prayer, God's Word, and worship, the Lord reminds me of all the ways He has been faithful to me. I write these down in my journal, recognizing that God can and will always bring me through my present circumstances.

I've always found that having an "attitude of gratitude" does a lot to change my anxious thoughts into the realization of just how much God has taken care of me in life. Write down in your journal the many, many blessings that the Lord has brought into your life. And make sure you think of the simple, day to day blessings that we—especially those of us in America—take for granted. A heart that is grateful has little room for fear and worry. Indeed, according to Tanya J. Peterson, "The brain can't respond to anxiety and gratitude at the same time, which means it's one or the other. We can feel anxious and other negative states, or we can feel grateful and all of the positive emotions that are associated with it."[9]

REMEMBER SELF-CARE

Our physical health is connected to our mental health. One of the best things you can do to redirect your anxiety is to get exercise. If you like going to the gym, do that. But it can also be as simple as going for a walk at the park, beach, trail, or in your town.

---

9.   Tanya J. Peterson, "Gratitude and Anxiety: To Be Less Anxious, Be More Grateful," *HealthyPlace* (blog), November 14, 2019, https://www.healthyplace.com/ blogs/anxiety-schmanxiety/2019/11/gratitude-and-anxiety-to-be-less-anxious-be-more-grateful.

Often when people are anxious, they either don't want to eat, or they eat a lot—usually food that is unhealthy and filled with sugar. Instead of this, eat balanced and nutritious meals. It not only helps your digestive system (which is usually affected by anxiety), but it gives you more energy, clearer thinking, and does a body good.

Clamp down on caffeine and get a good night's sleep. Caffeine is a stimulant, which is the last thing you want to drink when you're feeling anxious and need to get rest. Getting enough sleep does a body, mind, and soul a lot of good.

Take a break from work or your usual routine. Do something you enjoy, get a massage, take a day off, or, take some vacation days and go somewhere where you can unwind and relax.

When you redirect your anxiety by focusing on God and tending to your physical care, you will find your fear and worries will abate and that your faith will increase. George Müller, a Christian evangelist who lived in the 1800s, once said, "The beginning of anxiety is the end of faith, and the beginning of true faith is the end of anxiety."

LET GO OF THE NEED TO CONTROL

"Choose to let go—because there is a peace in realizing we aren't in control."

—Unknown

So, you must be in control? I understand. That was a problem I had to deal with early on in my life. I had my future mapped out. I had a plan, and everything needed to go according to my plan. When something happened to threaten my plan, I tried everything I could to bring about the outcome I wanted. How did it all work out? Well, I had severe anxiety, mountains of stress, strained relationships, and little to no peace. Oh, and *nothing* worked out as I had planned.

Do you want to know a little secret? You really aren't in control of much. That anxiety you carry around is merely the illusion of control. The more we "try" to control every aspect of our lives—our situations, circumstances, and outcomes—the more chaotic life becomes. When we seek to control everything (and everyone, I might add), we experience more anxiety, more stress, more mental and physical exhaustion, and a complete depletion of our emotions. In other words, we lose any sense of composure and peace, and suffer from having no self-regulation—making us someone that no one really wants to be around. The more you try to control your life, the more out of control your life will become. As Scripture reminds us, "The mind governed by the Spirit is life and peace."[10]

None of us are ever really in control. We like to think we are— we want to be the master of our own destiny. But neither you nor I have that kind of power. As Christians, our whole aim in life is to surrender our will to God's will. Faith and trust in Him allow us to bend our knee to the God who does have the power and authority over our life. Yet, as mere humans, we often struggle with "letting go and letting God."

Why do we do this? If we are honest, it's because we don't trust that God has our best interests at heart. We think we know better what we need, rather than the One who created us. But this is an illusion of control as well. I can tell you, as a pastor and a friend, that no one knows us better, including what we need or desire, than God himself. When you let go of the illusion of control, you not only let God be God in your life but you reap the peace, contentment, and assurance that only your Maker can give.

In God's mercy, He gives us opportunities to see that we are not in control. I've become a very calm person. Most people see me as being "chill" with my anxiety under control. That is until I get on an airplane. In that moment, I feel the realness that I am not in control. As soon as I sit in my seat, I start praying. I ask God to watch over the plane, to keep us from danger, to send His ministering angels to surround the plane, and to get us safely to our destination. Why do I do this? Because I know that I am not in control of that plane. Someone else is flying it, and I don't even know who that person is. Yet, when I drive my car, I feel like I am in control. I can take the roads I want and go as fast as I want. I'm not anxious when I am driving. Yet, the reality is that I've never had control over my travel, or anything else for that matter.

---

10.   Romans 8:6 (NIV).

Another reality check for me when it comes to the illusion of control is when I go in for surgery or a medical procedure. I've had many in my life. Before you go into surgery, you're always briefed on the possible complications that can take place during the procedure. Between that information and knowing I'm going to be under anesthesia the whole time, it's obvious that I am not in control. I realize that I'm at God's mercy. I'm in His hands, and I pray for Him to watch over me and take care of me while I'm out of it.

To have composure means you understand that you aren't in control, but God is, so you don't have to be upset about your situation or circumstances. Anything under God's control is never out of control. So, trust Him and relax.

STAY CALM UNDER PRESSURE

"A gentle answer turns away wrath, but a harsh word stirs up anger."

—***Proverbs 15:1 (NIV)***

Have you ever been in a public place, like a grocery store or restaurant, and watched someone lose their composure and have a meltdown right there in front of all to see? I sure have. In fact, I've seen parents lose it and just go off on their kids—screaming at them, demeaning them, and even hitting them—in a public space. I can't tell you how often I've wondered, "If they do this in public, what do they do at home?"

I grew up in a very dysfunctional home. There was a lot of yelling, screaming, arguing, slamming doors, and even worse. My dad had a bad temper—a problem with rage, in fact. And I was headed down that same path. I had a lot of anger toward my dad—a natural response to the often-abusive treatment I experienced from him throughout my childhood. When I turned 15 years old, my anger exploded, and my emotional state became terrible. My dad and I would not only fight verbally but physically as well.

After my dad passed away, I became aware that I didn't want to travel the same road that he did in his adult life. So, at age twenty-one, I gave my anger and hurt over to God. Out of the many important character traits I wanted to emulate, the ability to have composure was at the top of my list.

All through my childhood, I grew up with the desire to be the very opposite of my dad. It was a self-discipline process at first. But when I was taken aback by my own propensity toward anger and rage in my teen years, I realized that self-discipline alone was not enough. I needed a higher power to change my direction. God did just that.

Psychologists often talk about the generational cycles of abuse, mental illness, addiction, and other behaviors. The Bible refers to the same patterns as generational curses—the sins of the father playing out over many generations. I've got a friend who just went through a divorce because of his alcoholism. He couldn't stop drinking. His dad was an alcoholic as well, along with his father's father. There is a natural progression of these behaviors and others that are carried down through generational lines.

There is hope, however. We are not doomed to continue the cycle. I had a choice to stop the generational cycle with me. You have the same choice. Do you find yourself struggling with anger? Do you find it hard to keep your composure under pressure? Are you copying the same bad behaviors that you hated to see in that loved one while you were growing up?

There are two things you need to do to stop the unhealthy cycle of behaviors within your family. First, you must decide that this generational behavior stops with you. Second, you must start by doing the opposite of the injurious behavior. I grew up with angry, hurtful, and hateful words being yelled at me—day in and day out. So, I choose to stop that cycle by not having anger control me and my words. Then, I start living calmly and saying loving words.

There is a lot of power behind the realization that you need (and want) to stop the vicious cycle of behavior that has been handed down in your family. In many situations, professional counseling and help is needed. As a believer in Christ, my desire to not be like my earthly father was boosted by my desire to be like Jesus—to grow in His likeness. The power of God's spirit working in my life truly started to transform my heart, my thinking, and my behaviors. Before I was even married, I declared that the cycle was stopping with me and that I was not going to tear down my kids with my words but build them up with loving, peaceful, and reassuring words.

I'm happy to say that the abusive cycle stopped with me. When I got married, my wife and I made it a priority that love and peace would rule our home. There was no shouting, no yelling, and no abusive verbiage in our home. Our kids have never yelled at me or their mom. As teens, they never slammed doors, cussed at us, or told us that "they hated us," like most parents of teens have heard repeatedly. Because we made it a priority to emulate a peaceful (calm) and loving environment, our kids have grown into adults who have incredible composure under pressure.

Keeping your composure, especially under pressure, is both a choice and a learned ability. But it is also deeper than that. When your heart position is one of love and faith, rather than fear, anger, or worry, you can stay calm, trusting that God will work out everything in His perfect way and timing. Remember, having composure in your life creates peaceful and loving relationships. It truly is a key to unlocking your inner potential for kindness.

All of us recall a time when, under immense pressure, a leader, friend, pastor, or family member rose to a challenge while showing respect toward others and maintaining self-control and composure. That was an example of an unlocked and composed heart with a capacity for kindness that we all long to see evidence of more often. Be that person.

Key Four

UNLOCKING ACCEPTANCE

How to Open Our Hearts to People Who are Different
from Us, Defeat Our Own Biases, and Create Safe
Spaces for All People

*"Accept one another, then, just as Christ accepted you, in order to bring
praise to God."*

—Romans 15:7 (NIV)

Another key we need to find in our toolbox is the key that will
unlock our ability for acceptance, both of ourselves and others. This
key is engraved with a simple check mark. It's the one that will gain
us entry into the most tender part of our hearts, that place that longs
for validation for who we are. Too often, we can get locked up into
judging ourselves and others with standards that are rigid, rough,
and unmerciful. We can live our lives by rules instead of compassion.
We call this "self-righteousness."

Acceptance is the opposite of self-righteousness. Acceptance is
the ability to accept people as they are. Simply put, the act of acceptance means that we are to "welcome" people, not treating them
with any partiality because they look, act, think, or believe differently than we do. Throughout the Bible, we see that God welcomes
everyone who comes to Him. Jesus always extends acceptance and
kindness first. He never says, "First clean up your act, then come to
me." He values each person for what they have to offer.

Elizabeth Gilbert, in her book, *Committed: A Skeptic Makes Peace with Marriage*, says, "To be fully seen by somebody, then, and be loved anyhow—this is a human offering that can border on the miraculous." I love that quote because it aptly reflects the desire of every human being on this earth to be known; to be accepted as he or she is.

Jesus often ruffled the feathers of the religious leaders of His day—the Pharisees and Sadducees—because He welcomed, loved, and accepted everyone He met, especially those that the religious leaders had rejected—sinners, infirmed, outcasts, women, children, and all that were considered "less than," "vile," and "different."

It seems like a simple concept, doesn't it? Yet, we humans have a way of complicating everything.

LOVE YOUR NEIGHBOR

"If you really fulfill the royal law according to the Scripture, 'You shall love your neighbor as yourself,' you are doing well."

—James 2:8 (ESV)

The above Scripture tells us that "loving our neighbor" is a barometer on how well we are doing in our walk with God. I think there is no better time than today to ask ourselves, "How am I doing? Do I love my neighbor as myself? Do I treat others with the same acceptance, kindness, respect, and dignity that I desire for myself?"

Christians have been the target of major criticism from today's culture for their seeming lack of love for their neighbors. Let's be honest. Sometimes that criticism is well-deserved. We can come across as harsh, unaccepting, or judgmental toward people. The problem is that we too often think that we must compromise our convictions to love (accept) our neighbor, yet this is not the case at all.

None of us are given an "out" when it comes to the command to love our neighbors as ourselves. In fact, Jesus made it very clear just how important this command was to those who followed Him. He said, "'And you shall love the Lord your God with all your heart and with all your soul and with all your mind and with all your strength.'

The second is this: 'You shall love your neighbor as yourself.' There is no other commandment greater than these."[11]

God says that loving your neighbor is just as important as loving Him. In fact, if we love God with all our heart, soul, mind, and strength, then loving our neighbor is a natural by-product of our love for God. Ouch. Is it any wonder that our culture questions our faith when we are not showing love for our neighbor?

WHO IS MY NEIGHBOR?

"And behold, a lawyer stood up to put him to the test, saying, 'Teacher, what shall I do to inherit eternal life?' He said to him, 'What is written in the Law? How do you read it?' And he answered, 'You shall love the Lord your God with all your heart and with all your soul and with all your strength and with all your mind, and your neighbor as yourself.' And he said to him, 'You have answered correctly; do this, and you will live.'

"But he, desiring to justify himself, said to Jesus, 'And who is my neighbor?' Jesus replied, 'A man was going down from Jerusalem to Jericho, and he fell among robbers, who stripped him and beat him and departed, leaving him half dead. Now by chance a priest was going down that road, and when he saw him, he passed by on the other side. So likewise a Levite, when he came to the place and saw him, passed by on the other side. But a Samaritan, as he journeyed, came to where he was, and when he saw him, he had compassion. He went to him and bound up his wounds, pouring on oil and wine. Then he set him on his own animal and brought him to an inn and took care of him. And the next day he took out two denarii and gave them to the innkeeper, saying, 'Take care of him, and whatever more you spend, I will repay you when I come back.' Which of these three, do you think, proved to be a neighbor to the man who fell among the robbers?' He said, 'The one who showed him mercy.' And Jesus said to him, 'You go, and do likewise.'"[12]

I have always loved this parable. I think it calls attention to how we should treat people in today's culture. Notice that the lawyer was looking for an "out" when it came to loving his neighbor. It doesn't tell us whom the lawyer had a problem with or didn't like, but it was

11. Mark 12:30-31 (ESV).
12. Luke 10:25-37 (ESV).

clear that he did, and Jesus knew exactly what this young man was holding back. For Jesus to make it clear exactly who our neighbor is, he told a fascinating story that would cause them all to probably gasp, while driving the point home.

In that time, the religious leaders, the priests, and the Levites were among the most favored and honored in society. But the Samaritans were despised. They were considered the dregs of society; impure, immoral, and "less than." Notice how Jesus tells the story. A man travels along the road when he is robbed, beaten, and left for dead. A priest is traveling along the same route, but instead of going up to the man, he sees him and then "crosses the street" to the other side and keeps going. Next, a Levite (the tribe of Levi handled the priestly duties of the Temple—they managed the "church and worship service" so to speak) came near, and just like the priest, he crossed to the other side to avoid helping the man. Finally, Jesus says a Samaritan came along, and it was he who had compassion on the man, tending to his needs, and even going so far as to take him into town, getting him a place to stay and the care he needed.

Jesus then asked the lawyer who it was that ended up proving to be a neighbor to the injured man, and the lawyer answered correctly when he said, "The one who showed mercy."

I can only imagine that Jesus looked at this lawyer with compassion in his eyes, when he told him, "You go, and do likewise." Notice that Jesus took the most despised people group in that culture, the Samaritans, and made them the model of who a "neighbor" was and should be. He did this to show that there are no exceptions. Everyone is our neighbor. And in case we still don't get the message about loving our neighbor—let's face it, we can be kind of dense—Jesus also said, "Love your enemies, do good to those who hate you, bless those who curse you, pray for those who abuse you."

There are no "outs" when it comes to loving your neighbor, because even your "enemy" is to be loved. It's incredible that even in today's culture, we are still asking, "Who is my neighbor?" There is a popular image on social media that really captures the heart of who our neighbor is:

Love Thy Neighbor

Thy Homeless Neighbor
Thy Muslim Neighbor
Thy Black Neighbor
Thy Gay Neighbor
Thy White Neighbor
Thy Jewish Neighbor
Thy Christian Neighbor
Thy Atheist Neighbor
Thy Conservative Neighbor
Thy Progressive Neighbor
Thy Addicted Neighbor
Thy Immigrant Neighbor
Thy Transgender Neighbor

—*Author Unknown*

HOW CAN WE SHOW LOVE FOR OUR NEIGHBOR

"The good news is that there are no gatekeepers to Jesus. People try to be. Pastors, theologians, churches, and others police theology, enforce legalism, and criticize people's faith. But God loves everyone even when Christians don't."

—**Stephen Mattson,** *On Love and Mercy*

Loving our neighbor is less about agreeing with them and more about welcoming them—accepting them, walking in love toward them, and not judging them. I believe this plays out especially for those who are different from us in their sexual orientation or gender identity. I can have a biblical conviction that may be different from my LGBTQ neighbor, while living out another biblical conviction of loving them and accepting them as they are. I'm not going to judge, hate, or bully my LGBTQ neighbor. I'm going to love them as I want to be loved myself. Even though I don't fully understand my nieces and some of my daughter's friends who now identify as "them" or "him," I still love them, welcome them, and accept them as I always have. The bottom line is that when we accept people as they are, we are unlocking our ability to be extraordinarily kind.

So how can we practice kindness toward our neighbors—especially those who are of a different race, religion, orientation, ideology, or creed than us? I truly believe we need to be intentional in welcoming others into our lives. I have neighbors that live next door to me. One is an LGBTQ couple, and the other is a family that is committed to a faith different from mine. It's been a blessing to get to know them and call them friends. When my LGBTQ neighbors moved in, I went to their house and introduced myself, and welcomed them to our neighborhood. I gave them my contact information if they should ever need anything, and we ended up talking for twenty minutes that first night. The very next day, I was at the new pizza place in town and called my neighbors to see if I could bring them a pizza since they were amid a ton of boxes. They responded, "Oh, we'd love that." Later that week, we cooked dinner for them.

Accepting people—all people—opens the door to kindness, and when we are kind to those who live in our neighborhood, who ride on the train with us, who work with us, who we encounter during our day, and who we "do" life with, we will find it easy to show compassion, consideration, and acts of love.

LOVING OUR BLACK NEIGHBOR— ADDRESSING RACISM

I have been fighting racism most of my adult life. The fact that this is still entrenched in our society, and even in our churches, is something that frustrates and perplexes me. What's the remedy? Systemically, it's complicated. But as individuals, we each can make a difference by being accepting and inclusive in our friendships, our workplaces, our places of worship, our communities, and in our inner circles.

In 1994, when I was eighteen years old and in college, I invited my best friend to my church where I was the worship leader. A few times he sang with me and the worship team. Many of the worshippers told me they loved hearing my friend sing, but I also found out that some of the people didn't want him to ever come back. The next week some of these same people stood outside the doors, and when I walked up, they said, "We're not going to let that ["N-word"] in this church."

I was completely thunderstruck. Sure, my friend was African American. But this was 1994, and yet I felt like I had woken up that morning and been transported back to 1954. So, I met with my senior pastor, thinking that surely, he would be appalled by what these people were doing. Once I told him what was going on, he looked at me and said, "Greg, I want to ask you not to encourage your friend to come back to church." I was stunned. And just to make sure I heard him right, I asked, "Are you telling me not to invite my friend to church?" My senior pastor looked at me and said, "No, no, I'm not saying that. I'm just saying don't go out of your way to invite him—you know, don't encourage it."

I can't even share how I felt when hearing those words. But I had no problem replying to my pastor. I said, "You're a very weak leader." And I began to argue with him, quoting Scripture and telling him things that he should have known. Here I was, only eighteen years old, standing up to a senior pastor in his sixties. I found out that day what a weak leader looks like and what he does. This senior pastor didn't want any trouble from the racists in the church. He wanted to keep things calm, so he encouraged me not to invite my friend back. I knew without a doubt that Jesus would never have done that.

Every church I've served at, I have brought my friend with me because we have been confronting racism and breaking down barriers and walls since the 1990s. I've had the honor of pastoring a multi-ethnic church that was 50 percent black and 50 percent white. I've seen churches that had a beautiful unity, and I've seen churches that still struggle with racism. I've been passionate about this issue, especially as a Christian, and in some instances, I've experienced hate directed at me. I have spoken out about George Floyd, Breanna Taylor, and so many others who have been brutalized and died at the hands of white police officers. I have also marched numerous times with Black Lives Matters supporters. Many people have gotten upset with me. I've lost friendships, and I've been "unfriended" on Facebook and other social media channels. I've experienced the same reactions when fighting racism against Asian Americans as well. When I showed support for the "Stop Asian Hate" movement, many white friends got upset with me, argued with me, and I had to unfriend some on Facebook because they were so disrespectful and full of ignorant hate.

It's upsetting to see the amount of racism in our country. Personally, it is devastating to me when I see racist attitudes in the church. Christians should know better. The Bible affirms that all men and women are created equal, and all bear the image of God. Jesus preached about discrimination and commanded that we love our neighbor as ourselves and not to judge others, especially when based on appearance. As it says in the Bible:

> Then God said, "Let us make mankind in our image, in our likeness, so that they may rule over the fish in the sea and the birds in the sky, over the livestock and all the wild animals, and over all the creatures that move along the ground." So, God created mankind in his own image, in the image of God he created them; male and female he created them.[13]

Alveda King, the niece of Martin Luther King Jr., said, "Racism springs from the lie that certain human beings are less than fully human. It's a self-centered falsehood that corrupts our minds into believing we are right to treat others as we would not want to be treated."[14]

ACCEPTANCE DOESN'T TOLERATE "BULLYING"

Unlocking acceptance is a key that helps us behave kindly to all we meet. When we lack an attitude of acceptance toward others, we can fall prey to the insidious act of bullying. A bully is habitually

---

13. Genesis 1:26-27 (NIV).
14. Alveda King (@AlvedaCKing), Twitter, 9:42 a.m, June 27, 2019, https://twitter.com/alvedacking/status/1144254692240834561.

cruel, insulting, or threatening to others who are weaker, smaller, different, marginalized, or vulnerable.

I'm well acquainted with what it feels like to be bullied. Though I'm a big guy now, standing at 6'5", when I was a kid, I was very little, and I became a target for bullies. Whether it was name calling, pranks at my expense, or outright physical violence, bullying led to a significant amount of trauma and anxiety. I dreaded going to school every day.

Bullying is something that unfortunately happens too much in this country. It's not just young people who bully but adults as well. The problem, which has invaded social media too, has escalated so much that not a week goes by that we don't read about an individual committing suicide (or attempting suicide) due to the harassment they have received from bullies. What steps can be taken to curb bullying in our nation?

Some schools use what is called the Promise Program to train students against bullying. This program was adapted from *The Juice Box Bully: Empowering Kids to Stand Up for Others*, a book by Bob Sornson and Maria Dismondy. The following Promises, as they've become known, are something everyone—kids and adults—can all learn from:

- I will speak up instead of acting as a bystander.

- I choose to participate in activities that don't involve teasing.

- I forgive others if they make poor choices.

- I model good behavior.

- I accept others for their differences.

- I include others in group situations.

- I will talk to an adult when there is a situation I cannot manage on my own.

- I am powerful in making a difference in my school, neighborhood, and community.

Bullying is the result of a lack of acceptance of others. We must unlock acceptance to be kind to others and to create an environment of respect and dignity for all human beings. I saw a quote recently that sums up everything I've said in this chapter in a simple way:

"We could all take a lesson from crayons:
Some are sharp, some are beautiful,
some have weird names,
and all are different colors,
but they still learn to live in the same box."

—Author Unknown

Are you interested in anti-bullying campaigns? Grassroots movements such as #BeKind (2bekind.com) and Dignity Revolution (dignitypledge.com) have popped up in response to the increased bullying environment in schools and communities nationwide.

Bullying, like other forms of discrimination and nonacceptance, comes most often from a feeling of superiority, low self-esteem, inner anger, or self-loathing. The more we learn to accept ourselves, our mistakes, our weaknesses, and our differences, the more we will be attuned to treating others with equal respect, honor, dignity, and love.

Key Five

UNLOCKING REST

How to Prioritize Sleep, Rethink Wellness, and Stay in
Good Spirits

"Come to me, all who labor and are heavy laden, and I will give you rest."
—Matthew 11:28 (ESV)

*According to a Greek legend, in ancient Athens a man noticed the great
storyteller, Aesop, playing childish games with some little boys. He laughed and
jeered at Aesop, asking him why he wasted his time in such frivolous activity.
Aesop responded by picking up a bow, loosening its string, and placing it on
the ground. Then he said to the critical Athenian, "Now answer the riddle, if
you can. Tell us what the unstrung bow implies."
The man looked at it for several moments but had no idea what point Aesop
was trying to make. Aesop explained, "If you keep the bow always bent, it
will break eventually; but if you let it go slack, it will be more fit for use
when you want it."
People are also like that. That's why we all need to take time to rest.*
—Bible.org, "Meaning of the Unstrung Bow"

I love this story about Aesop. It's a great reminder of what can
happen to us when we don't take the time to care for ourselves, which
includes rest and wellness for our body, mind, and soul. Without
paying attention to self-care, we will indeed break.

49

The next key we draw from our toolbox will unlock our ability to rest, to break from the busyness of life, the excessive expectations, and the exhaustion we feel when we push ourselves relentlessly. We cannot possibly tap into our secret well of kindness when we drive ourselves like bulls. Being kind first to ourselves and then to others will come from not a place of tension but always a place of rest. The symbol on our key of rest is a symbol found in music. It's *selah*, which means "pause, a break, a stop, a rest."

When was the last time you woke up totally refreshed? For too many of us, the stress of life, combined with our lack of self-care, zaps our ability to do our best, be our best, and enjoy our daily lives. In our driven culture, we emphasize "doing" often to the extreme, creating uncontrolled stress, elevated frustration, irritation, and anger, which leads to mental and physical exhaustion. All the striving, the long work hours, and the lack of rest take a toll on our mental and physical health.

Consider for a moment the fact that

- 1 million Americans have a heart attack each year.

- 13 billion doses of tranquilizers, barbiturates, and amphetamines are prescribed yearly.

- 8 million Americans have stomach ulcers.

- An estimated 50,000 stress-related suicides take place each year.

- We have 12 million alcoholics in our country.

Vance Havner, author and old-time preacher and revivalist once said, "Unless we come apart and rest a while, we may just plain come apart."

REST NEEDS TO BE A PRIORITY

"If you do not rest, it negatively impacts your performance and consequently, your business. You're more focused, you're more creative, and you're more productive when you're well-rested."

—**Michael Hyatt,** *Free to Focus*

The key to mental, physical, and spiritual health is rest. Rest can be defined as "peace, ease, or refreshment" and can be applied by getting enough sleep, having sufficient time off or away from your work, taking time to enjoy things in life, and having "down time" or "alone time" to relax your mind and body. Talking about the importance of rest, Ben Nussbaum and Mallory Corbin's share the following story in an article published in *Spirituality & Health Magazine*,

> Despite a high-pressure job producing films, Tracee Stanley had everything under control. Prioritizing her own wellbeing made her more effective and efficient at work—which gave her time and space to prioritize her own wellbeing. "I remember feeling very blissful," she says. "I had ten different projects I was working on that I was excited about." The company's owner interrupted her bliss by stopping her in the hallway and asking her why she wasn't running around frantically like everyone else in the office. "Oh, this is so interesting," she remembers thinking, "You are so invested in grind culture that you don't see I'm more productive than anyone in the office—because I'm rested. You expect to be able to see chaos."[15]

Though there are prominent cultures in the world that esteem and make time for daily rest, there are other societies, including that of the United States, that esteem an over-the-top hard work ethic (meaning, workaholic status) as a means of success. But this mentality, which negates the need for rest, has resulted in broken relationships, burn out, ill health, and escalated mental illness. There have been strides in the United States toward embracing a lifestyle of balance. Wellness has become a prominent industry and the 2020 pandemic ushered in remote working. People are starting to realize that having an excellent work ethic includes the need for rest.

What about you—are you prioritizing the need for "rest" in your life? Do you still need convincing of this fact?

---

15. Ben Nussbaum and Mallory Corbin, "The REST Story," *Spirituality & Health Magazine*, Mar. 2021, https://www.magzter.com/stories/Religious-Spiritual/Spirituality-Health/The-REST-Story.

IF GOD PRIORITIZES REST, SO SHOULD YOU

The Bible has a lot to say about the need for rest. Right from the beginning, we see that God established a day of rest after He had fulfilled His work of creation. "So God blessed the seventh day and made it holy, because on it God rested from all his work that he had done in creation."[16] I love the fact that God is the originator of "rest." Chew on that for a while. If God ordained it and rested Himself, that should banish any feeling of shame or weakness that some dole out when people strive for a work-life balance.

Throughout Scripture, rest and wellness are prescriptions, not only for the people of Israel through the Sabbath day but for the Gentiles as well. When Jesus walked the earth and held His public ministry, He placed a great importance on rest. He often departed away from the crowds in solitude to pray and get needful sleep. In the Old and New Testaments, we see many examples of God telling his prophets to rest and to eat to have strength. And when Jesus healed people, He would direct others to get them something to eat, so they regained their strength.

Is it any wonder that the author of "rest" said, "Come to me, all who labor and are heavy laden, and I will give you rest. Take my yoke upon you, and learn from me, for I am gentle and lowly in heart, and you will find rest for your souls."[17]

THE POWER OF EIGHTS IN REST AND SELF-CARE

I have been talking across the country about the Power of the Eights. Before I tell you what that is, let me tell you how I came to discover this simplistic but profound and healthy way to balance the time in my life.

I have long struggled with back pain. My back issues have included a myriad of troubles, including bulging discs. Years ago, I

---

16. Genesis 2:3 (ESV).
17. Matthew 11:28-29 (ESV).

woke up every day in tremendous pain. I didn't have a sports injury, and I didn't physically do anything to injure my back. Yet, every single day, I would wake up in excruciating pain. I went to several doctors, and I would see my chiropractor and get adjusted every day to get some relief. On one occasion, my chiropractor asked me, "Hey, Greg, what kind of mattress do you have?" And I said, "Why do you ask?" He said, "Well, I don't know if you realize this, but you spend a third of your life asleep. Eight hours a day in a 24- hour span is spent asleep in the bed. So, invest in a good one."

That should have been a no-brainer, right? But I have to say, it became revolutionary for me. So, I went out and bought a new bed and invested in a great mattress and it's really helped not only my quality of sleep but to reduce my back pain as well.

As you might have guessed from my story, the power of the eights refers to our 24-hour day. Each person on this planet has a 24-hour day—a block of time by which we live our daily lives. Now take your 24-hour day and, like a pie graph, divide it into thirds so that you have three 8-hour blocks of time for each day. For many people, one block of 8 hours will be applied to work, career, or schooling. Another 8-hour block of time can be applied to your home life, your social life, your self-care, and so forth. And then, the last 8-hour block of time is applied to your needed rest, specifically, your sleep mode. Why is this breakdown of your 24-hour day so important? This is where you find your work-life-rest balance, my friends. And if you're going to be healthy, have vitality, and be of good disposition in body, mind, and spirit, you must prioritize rest and find balance in your 24-hour day.

SELF-CARE INCLUDES YOUR MENTAL HEALTH TOO

"It shouldn't take a pandemic to convince people to put their mental health above their careers. In the long run, the choice between success and well-being is a false dichotomy. The best way to achieve your goals is to lead a life that invigorates you—not one that drains you."

—*Adam Grant, Twitter, Jun 30, 2022*

I'm passionate about mental health. I have gone public with my story, speaking about my struggle with bipolar disorder and anxiety. I have also served as a resource over the years to not only help people in these areas but to train church leaders so that they know how to minister to those in their congregations that struggle with mental illness, as well as to get help for themselves if they struggle with their own mental health in their life. Whether it's depression, anxiety, bipolar disorder, borderline personality disorder, ADHD, or something else, mental illness is finally getting well-deserved attention. Stigmas are being torn down, people are opening up, and help and resources are more readily available than they were ten years ago. There are also far more people today struggling with mental illness than at any other time in our country.

The pandemic was rough on mental health. Between isolation, fear, anxiety, and a change in how we worked, shopped, did business, and went to school, it's no wonder that there has been a "second pandemic" going on in America—one involving mental health.

I could write an entire series of books on mental health, but right now, I want to focus on the need for rest and work-life balance when it comes to your mental health. In all truth, every human being struggles with mental health. You may not have a disorder or need to take medicine as a lot of us do, but you do need to take care of your mental health. Stress, pressure, fear, anxiety, and a lack of balance in your life all contribute negatively to your mind, whether it be your thoughts, your mood, your attitude, or your behavior. That's why rest is one of the keys to unlocking your potential for kindness. If you don't incorporate rest in your life, you will be cranky, irritable, and on a short fuse with people rather than being kind. Let's look at the three 8-hour segments in your life to see just how important rest and balance is to your well-being.

THE IMPORTANCE OF SLEEP

On average, adults need 8 hours of sleep. Though that can vary a bit, it's the American medical Association's suggested sleep time to maintain a healthy lifestyle for both body and mind. A good night's sleep plays a significant role in mental health. The best thing we can do when it comes to rest and self-care is to have a healthy sleep pattern. Too many people struggle with getting a good night's sleep. In what my therapist calls good sleep hygiene, the following points are tips on creating a healthy sleep pattern:

1. **Have a set bedtime and wake-up time.** Try to go to bed the same time each night and try to wake up the same time each morning. This simple pattern will help your body adjust to a regular night's sleep. I do this and I can say it's really helped my mental health as well as increased my energy levels during the day.

2. **Create a routine.** A healthy routine coincides with your sleep pattern. At bedtime, you want to wind down, so it's a suitable time to read a book or journal about your day. In the morning, you want to start your day off in a positive way. When I wake up in the morning I go downstairs and put the TV on, and instead of watching the news, I watch worship videos on YouTube. After making my cup of coffee, I usually read Scripture and journal my thoughts that morning. Everyone is different—so, establish your own routine for bedtime and for waking up. Keep it positive. You don't want to load your mind with anything disruptive or agitating prior to going to sleep, or upon waking up first thing in the morning.

3. **Shelve the electronics.** If you're looking at your phone, tablet, or television in bed at night, you're going to stay awake because the screen itself charges your mind and gets your body revved up in the same way caffeine does. If you need to wind down, read a book, which will help you get sleepy in a natural way.

4. **Cut off caffeine and sugar in the evening.** This should be obvious, but I know many people who have a soda, a cup of coffee, or dessert in the evening and then have trouble sleeping at night. You need to establish a cut-off time that

works best for your body and stick with it. Some people I know don't have any caffeine or sugar after 4pm, and others set their cut-off time at 8pm. If you aren't sure what time to set, take a week to experiment by trying various times. If you are able, cutting out caffeine and sugar is a tremendous help in controlling anxiety.

5. **Avoid alcohol before bed.** Just as with caffeine and sugar, alcohol before bed can mess with your anxiety and have a negative impact on your sleep.

6. **Save high intensity exercise for earlier in the day.** If you want to wake up and go for a jog, workout at the gym, or ride a bike that's a terrific way to invigorate and build up your energy, but that routine too close to bedtime may destroy your ability to get a good night's sleep.

7. **Keep your bed just for sleeping.** In other words, don't use it as an opportunity to catch up on work, play video games, or watch television. Your mind needs to know that when you lay down at night in your bed, it's time to wind down and sleep. This is an important part of a healthy sleep pattern.

8. **Have a comfortable sleep environment.** I learned this important lesson from my chiropractor—invest in the right mattress and pillow that fits your body. When you don't have the support you need from your bedding, you can struggle with a stiff neck and sore muscles. It's common for people to skimp on bedding items, but considering we spend a third of our life sleeping, it's worth investing in the right bed, mattress, pillows, and bedding to give you a good night's sleep.

9. **Limit (or stop all-together) naps in the day.** When I say to limit (preferably stop all-together) nap time in the day, I am not referring to "power naps" that only last 15 minutes at your desk. Since so many people are still working remote

from their homes, I'm talking about taking a siesta on the couch or even in your bed that can last an hour or more. By doing this, you will not be as tired in the evening. It's far better to be ready to fall asleep when it's time for bed as it will assure that you do get a good night's sleep.

Never underestimate the power of a good night's sleep when it comes to your wellness and mental health. For those of you who struggle with anxiety like I do, a lot of times you go straight to thinking you need more medicine, or that you need to see the therapist more times per week to subdue anxiety. However, if you would just go back to something as simple and as basic as sleep hygiene, you'll find that it will help you very much in your quest for living a less anxious life.

THE IMPORTANCE OF HAVING TIME TO RELAX

We all need time to recharge our batteries. And, depending on your personality, sometimes you need to learn how to relax. Here are some tips to help you set aside time to truly relax in the course of your day:

1. **Do something you enjoy.** Never underestimate the need for "fun" in your life. Now, unless your fun is "trying to win a triathlon," doing something you enjoy often is the best way to relax. For some, gardening may be your relaxer, or sitting in your beach chair at the beach. For others, perhaps you have a hobby that you enjoy, or you love to go antiquing.

2. **Do something that calms you.** What in your life brings you peace and calm? As a Christian man, when I spend time in prayer, reading the Bible, or listening to worship music, I find peace that passes all understanding. What about you? Maybe you like to meditate, do yoga, or listen to classical music? I know many pet owners who find great

peace when taking their dogs for a walk. Are you a nature lover? Walk some trails, go to the beach or the lake, or find an open field and just lay in it.

3. **Spend time with your family and friends.** If you're married, it's important to spend time with your spouse and children. Do something fun with them—watch a movie, get ice cream, go to the park, have a date night—and find relaxation being with the ones you love. If you're single, go out to dinner with a friend, go to a coffee house to chat, see a movie, or take an evening walk. Spending intentional time with friends and loved ones works wonders on your mental health.

THE IMPORTANCE OF HAVING BOUNDARIES IN YOUR WORK SCHEDULE

Finally, to prioritize rest and relaxation into your life, it is necessary to have boundaries when it comes to your work or career. The power of the 8s helps you to establish boundaries as to what you do with your three 8-hour segments of time per day. There is nothing wrong with a hard work ethic until it crosses the line of molding you into a workaholic. If you're working day and night, bringing work home all the time, and often working on the weekend, then you're spending the majority of your 24-hour day on work, which is unhealthy.

The healthiest way to live is by appropriating 8-hours for sleep, 8-hours for work, and 8-hours for family, social, rest/relaxation, and "alone time." I'm not saying that you can never bring work home, work on a weekend, or work late one night. However, what I am saying is that you need to develop a pattern of living a balanced life by setting boundaries on your work life to a three 8-hour segment per day, even if you must work a touch more than that here and there.

I think you can agree that it's easy to spend a much larger chunk of our time working. But it's not healthy. Prioritize your tasks at work in such a way that you can finish what you need to do in your 8-hour day. Even if you have to work overtime occasionally or bring some work home or work on a weekend here and there, let it be the exception and not the norm. Only you can set boundaries in your life, but when you do (and I highly recommend following the Power of the Eights), you will find a far better version of yourself (one that is kind, by the way) because you're relaxed, rested, and healthier.

Key Six

UNLOCKING WISDOM

How to Only Pick Battles Worth Fighting For

"If any of you lacks wisdom, let him ask God, who gives generously to all without reproach, and it will be given him."

—James 1:5 (ESV)

We can all use a big dose of wisdom, don't you agree? People often think that wisdom and intelligence are one in the same. But they are not. In fact, there's a big difference between the two. Someone can have a high IQ, yet at the same time not be wise. Or, someone with meager means can be an incredibly wise person. In fact, the Bible tells us that anyone can be wise by simply asking God to give them wisdom.

So what is *wisdom*? Wisdom is the ability to discern inner qualities and relationships—to be wise means you have insight, good sense, and keen judgment. Another definition, which I have always thought shows the wisdom of God's creation, is that wisdom has to do with understanding and accepting the fundamental nature of things in life.

So, the next key we need to unlock the fences of defensiveness and contention around us is the key to unlocking our inner wisdom. This key looks a lot like a tree with roots deeply planted within our sense of self, our faith in God, and our identity as beloved. When impulsivity, folly, or imperviousness begin to enter into our lives, we can not only lose our own sense of direction but can be blind to the way our decisions affect others, resulting in unkind behaviors and disrespect. By unlocking and allowing wisdom to infiltrate our lives, we will be able to live the way Jesus meant us to live, as kind, loving, compassionate people of God.

The Bible says, "A person's wisdom yields patience; it is to one's glory to overlook an offense."[18] Today, people get outraged over every minor irritation. I must say, social media makes this especially easy with little accountability. As we all know, our culture is deeply divided, and the lack of even being able to disagree agreeably seems to have faded into the sunset. Have you noticed that people's fuses are increasingly shorter? Some people are quick to anger and slow to listen, which is the exact opposite of God's character.

To be kind, especially in our polarizing world, one needs to be wise. That means we need to know when to speak up and when to be quiet. We need to know how to choose our words wisely instead of letting our uncontrolled emotions blurt out words that hurt others. It means that we are peacemakers—preserving relationships instead of bulldozing people down. It also means that we need to know how to pick our battles and not be combative over any slight irritation or difference in opinion. And having wisdom means we shower people with grace and mercy rather than having a self-righteous or judgmental attitude.

I like what Rick Warren said about this when he stated, "We're all like tubes of toothpaste. Whatever's inside of you comes out when you're squeezed by immense pressure. Are you filled with anger or graciousness?"

What about you? Are you filled with anger or grace? Do you consider yourself wise, or are you found lacking in this area?

---

18. Proverbs 19:11 (NIV).

THE SOUND OF SILENCE: USING WISDOM WHEN IT COMES TO YOUR WORDS

"A soft answer turns away wrath, but a harsh word stirs up anger."

—Proverbs 15:1 (ESV)

How do you react when somebody looks at you the wrong way or says something the wrong way? Do you hold your tongue, or do you give that person a tongue-lashing? Think about this for a moment. Are you easily offended? Do you feel justified in giving people a "piece of your mind"? Wisdom asks, "Is it worth addressing what they just said or how they looked at me? The Bible says that a fool blurts out many words while a wise person listens. Someone once said, "You are most powerful when you are most silent. People never expect silence. They expect words, motion, defense, and offense. They expect you to leap into the fray. They are ready, fists up, words hanging and leaping from their mouths. Do they expect silence? No."

Let's face it, our instinct is to defend ourselves at all costs. We want to give people a piece of our mind when they offend us or even just disagree with us. But a wise person overlooks an offense.

Is there any doubt that we can all use some wisdom? This is something that our culture needs desperately. We are far too easily offended. We are far too volatile. And we are far too inclined to stir people up rather than be peacemakers.

Instead of the sound of "verbal vomit" pouring forth from our mouths, we need to appreciate the sound of silence. That's what Jesus did. Scripture says, "When he was accused by the chief priests and the elders, he gave no answer. Then Pilate asked him, 'Don't you hear the testimony they are bringing against you?' But Jesus made no reply, not even to a single charge—to the great amazement of the governor."[19]

If anyone had a reason to lash out with words, it was Jesus. Though completely innocent, He had been set up by Judas, plotted against by the religious leaders who despised and rejected Him, and

---

19.   Matthew 27:12-14 (NIV).

falsely accused by "witnesses" who had been paid off by powerful leaders. The very people Jesus loved, fed, cared for, and healed turned against Him. And yet, He remained silent. Offense after offense was hurled at Him, but He didn't defend Himself. Even on the cross, while the crowds looked on and mocked Him, Jesus showed His grace and compassion, saying, "Father forgive them, for they know not what they do."[20]

When we have wisdom, we put a filter on our mouth—either remaining silent or choosing words that diffuse the situation. The Bible says, "Let your conversation be always full of grace, seasoned with salt, so that you may know how to answer everyone."[21]

WHEN IT COMES TO DIFFICULT PEOPLE—CHOOSE WISDOM, EMPATHY, AND GRACE

Do you have any "difficult" people in your life? At work, in your family, or even at your place of worship? How do you react when someone is angry, cranky, or judgmental—especially when you're at a store, at a restaurant, or any public space? Rick Warren once said, "My patience with mean or angry or judgmental folks increased greatly when a friend taught me to stop asking (in my mind), 'What's wrong with you?' and start asking (in my mind), 'What happened to you?'" I really like this quote from Rick Warren. When you come across somebody that's rough around the edges—grumpy, callous, mean, rude, or just tough to be around—take a deep breath, pause, and then ask yourself, "What happened to that person," rather than angrily thinking, "What is wrong with that person?" By doing this, you not only calm yourself down, but you start feeling empathy toward that difficult person, and you respond with grace.

If it's someone you know (and not a stranger), you can even start a conversation with them by saying, "So, tell me your story; tell me about your life." We need to realize that everyone has a story. And most people, if not all, have a messy story. Think about your own

20. Luke 23:34 (ESV).
21. Colossians 4:6 (NIV).

life—the difficulties, the good, bad, and the ugly. When you engage the difficult person in conversation and show interest and grace, you may start to see the rough exterior layer start to come off.

When we mentally think, "What in the world is wrong with you," we often incorrectly size up and assume many bad things about the person. Yet, the reality is that maybe nothing is wrong with them. Maybe, instead, they're a beautiful human being that has gone (or is going through) something exceedingly difficult in life.

So how should we react to difficult people? The Bible gives clear direction when it says, "Put on then, as God's chosen ones, holy and beloved, compassionate hearts, kindness, humility, meekness, and patience, bearing with one another and, if one has a complaint against another, forgiving each other; as the Lord has forgiven you, so you also must forgive."[22]

THE PROBLEM WITH ANGER

"He who is slow to anger is better than the mighty, and he who rules his spirit than he who takes a city."

—Proverbs 16:32 (ESV)

I grew up in a home with a lot of anger. As I said in an earlier chapter, my dad had a horrific temper. And as a teenager, at the age of fifteen, I expressed a lot of my own anger. Right after I found out about my dad's other family, I responded with rebellion and acting out—being mean back to my dad and fighting with him. I didn't want to hear from him because he had lied to us about his other family. So, I pushed back. But I found, as I went on to college, that the anger, the rebellion, the cursing, and the vileness was destroying me. I didn't like whom I had become. In fact, I realized that I was behaving just as my dad. It was at that point that I gave my anger to God—I asked Him to take it away and make me a gentle soul and a peacemaker. And that's precisely what God did—He transformed my heart, which transformed my mind, which resulted in changed behaviors.

---

22.   Colossians 3:12-13 (ESV).

I became intentional about where I would put my time, effort, and energy. Think about this for a moment. It takes a lot of effort and energy to be angry. And the result of that effort is never a positive outcome. So instead, I'm going to put my time, effort, and energy into remaining peaceful with people—choosing to be kind when I could snap back and choosing to be gracious when I could respond in anger. Are you thinking this sounds easier said than done?

There are four important steps to unlock wisdom and maintain your cool:

1. Seek God: First and foremost, seek God. Ask Him for wisdom and to transform your heart from a position of anger to a position of peace.

2. Be Intentional: Choose to be intentional in putting your time, effort, and energy into remaining peaceful with people. The more you choose how you want to respond, the better your relationships will be.

3. Breathe: There's something immensely powerful about focused breathing. When you're cognitively aware of your breathing (deep breath in, a slow exhale out), it helps you to cool down and relax.

4. Push Pause: When irritated, instead of reacting and flying off the handle, pause and take time to think. Is this really a battle I want to fight? This is where wisdom plays into your decision. Because a wise person would say, "No, that's not a battle I want to fight. That's not worth my time, effort, or energy. It's not worth losing my cool and my peace."

CONTROLLING REACTIVE ANGER—THE WISDOM TO CHOOSE YOUR BATTLES

"A wrathful man stirs up discord, but one who is slow to anger appeases strife."

—*Proverbs 15:18 (WEB)*

If we are honest with ourselves, most of the situations or circumstances that irritate us and make us angry are not major battles. They may be irritations, but in the grand scheme of life, they are not worthy of our time, energy, and angry reaction. For example, my wife can get angry over the fact that I didn't unload the dishwasher or make the bed. Yes, these things are legitimately irritating to her. But, as we commonly do in our marriage, we will both say to each other, "Choose your Battles. Is this really the hill you want to die on?"

Whether you're dealing with a slow person at checkout in a grocery store or pharmacy, waiting in a never-ending line at the DMV, or driving on the road and getting cut off or tailgated, you need to determine if this is really the battle you want to wage. Yes, these things are all irritations, but do they really deserve you becoming extremely angry in anger? Be honest. Wisdom tells you that these things are not worth getting worked up and angry about. In fact, in all these situations (and most others), wisdom encourages you to be calm and less engaged in frivolous arguments.

It's important to realize that the person you're irritated with could be sick, they could be tired, or stressed, they could be having a bad day, or they may be experiencing a difficult circumstance in their life. So instead of confronting them or biting their head off, you will show them grace and just move on with your day. It's the wisdom of knowing how to choose your battles.

Now there are times in life when you must speak up for something essential and stand for what you believe in. These are the hills to die on—something that's morally right, like ethical treatment of people, or something morally wrong, like human trafficking or racism. These are things you want to speak out on or take a stand about, but when it comes to frivolous things—things that aren't going to matter at the end of the day (or at the end of your life), you want to be quick to listen, slow to anger, and eager to show grace.

When you and your spouse (or friend / family member) have a disagreement about something irritating, can you let it go or come to a compromise? Instead of putting your stake in the ground, digging your heels in, and saying, "I'm not budging," you can choose to find a compromise that is agreeable to both parties. It's always far better to find common ground than to choose to die on a hill over something that may be irritating but not significant.

POLITICAL DIVIDES AND OTHER DISAGREEMENTS: THE WISDOM OF THE THIRD OPTION

Since the beginning of human government, there have always been political divides and disagreements in the body politic. Yet, at least in my lifetime, I have not before witnessed such deep political divides, polarization, and demonizing of one another as we see happening in our culture today. How did it get this way? There's no doubt that a big part of the problem is that we get so extremely set in our ways that we don't want to accept another person's point of view or opinion. In fact, we don't even want to listen to each other's viewpoint. Instead of trying to find common ground with one another, we instead choose to vilify the "other side" as if we alone have the right answers for every issue our country faces. This has created an "us versus them" mentality in our government, the public square, and sadly, even in our own families or home.

Too often our politics are rigid—it's a black and white, all or nothing, one party or the other driven narrative that caters to and attracts the extremes, leaving no room for moderation or compromise. We have seen what this has done up close and personal. People can't even talk about their political beliefs without getting mean, angry, or even hateful. So, what do we do? How do we keep peace with those that think far differently than we do when it comes to politics? There is wisdom in the third option. The third option seeks to find a common cause, concern, or experience—a middle ground that is shared by both people. No matter how different people can be in their beliefs, it is our shared humanity where we can find common ground. It can be love for our kids, a passion for sports, art, books, business, or more.

Do you know what I have found when taking the third option? We have a lot more in common with people than we think we do. When you start having conversations about life and what you want, not only for yourselves, but for your kids, your community, and the world, you realize that we all want kindness, civility, peace, and be a part of the greater good. Often our goals are the same, but our methodology is what we have at odds.

I used to always say to my children and others, "I don't care about your religious beliefs or your political beliefs, at the end of the day just be a decent human being and contribute to the greater good."

MAKING A CHANGE FOR THE BETTER: BECOMING THE PERSON GOD WANTS YOU TO BE

"But you were washed, you were sanctified, you were justified in the name of the Lord Jesus Christ and by the Spirit of our God."

—1 Corinthians 6:11 (ESV)

Have you ever given anything over to God? Do you struggle with anger? Do you find it challenging to show grace or have mercy on people? I encourage you to give these areas over to God. Meaning do a 180-degree turnaround (a biblical definition of repentance) and decide that you don't want to be angry anymore or filled with hostility towards people. Instead, you turn towards God and say, "I give it to you. I'm turning away from it and coming back to a place of peace, a place of calm, and a place of wisdom. Set a guard over my mouth so that my words bring life and not death."

God is faithful to transform you into the person He wants you to be. Not only will He transform the way you talk to people, but also the way you talk to yourself. Negative self-talk is not from God. If I walk around saying, "I'm a loser," that's from the enemy. Renounce that in the name of Jesus and say, "I'm not a loser. I'm a child of God, I'm loved. I'm chosen, and I'm forgiven."

Take God's promises and walk them out in freedom and healing. Don't believe the lie that you will always be angry. Or think, 'My dad was a drunk, so I'll be a drunk.' Stop that generational curse mentality. Instead, say, "This ends with me." I did that myself. I was not going to have my kids growing up in a dysfunctional home. I was intentional about having them grow up in a peaceful and loving home.

Andy Stanley authored a great book called, *The Principle of the Path*, which says that when you intentionally set out in a specific direction that's where you're going to end up. So, if you set out on a direction of health and fitness, you're going to end up healthy. You can say all day that you wish you were in better shape, but that will not get you anywhere. It's when you are intentional to set out on a path of health and fitness that you will reap a healthy lifestyle.

You must make a choice to intentionally forge the path where you want to end up. For example, from the very beginning of the first chapter on unforgiveness, I had a choice to make—I could be bitter or get better. And I definitely wanted to get better. I was not going to live my life as a bitter old man around my spouse, kids, friends, and coworkers.

It takes wisdom to realize the principle of the path that you want for your life. I knew I wanted to live a peaceful, happy, cheerful, kind, fun, and joyous life. We want to choose joy. We want to live a peaceful, kind life.

None of us know the number of our days on this earth. My wife's cousin died at the age of 26. Though her life was short, it was beautiful. She was sweet, kind, and a shining light to all. She is dearly missed. And yet some people live until they're very old, but they're not missed by anybody. They die a lonely death, and nobody comes to the funeral. In the same way, some people come into a room and drain the energy out of it, while others come into a room and light it up.

How do you want to live? What do you want to be known for? There's wisdom in the Principle of the Path . . . and it's time to take that first step.

FOR FURTHER READING

Francis P. Martin, *Hung by the Tongue: What You Say Is What You Get*

Andy Stanley, *The Principle of the Path: How to Get from Where You Are to Where You Want to Be*

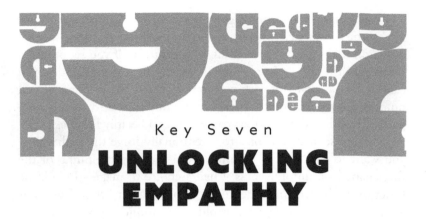

Key Seven

UNLOCKING EMPATHY

How to Overcome Your Empathy Barriers and Truly Connect with People

"Rejoice with those who rejoice, and weep with those who weep. . . . Live in harmony with one another."

—Romans 12:15-16 (ESV)

Ginger Sprouse is one of those people who wants to do more for the homeless than simply give them a meal. One homeless man in particular caught Ginger's attention when he sat in the same spot nearly every day near her cooking class business. She learned that his name was Victor, and he had a mental illness. He wanted to wait in that one spot every day in the hope that his mother would find him, because that's where he'd last seen her.

Ginger befriended Victor, talking to him on her coffee breaks and learning about his life, including the fact that he'd been homeless for about 10 years and unable to find his mother for the last three.

In December 2016, Ginger decided to take Victor into her home and started a Facebook campaign, known as "This Is Victor," to raise money to help get Victor on his feet. She gave him a job in the kitchen of her business and even helped him see his mom again. She plans on helping Victor for the rest of his life if that's what he needs.[23]

---

23. Ginger Sprouse, *Kinda Like Grace* (Nashville: Thomas Nelson, 2019).

GUGUGUG

Empathy, in a simplified definition, is the ability to understand and share the feelings of another. However, it really is a great deal more than that. Empathy is the ability to emotionally understand what other people feel, see things from their point of view, and imagine yourself in their place. When you see another person suffering, like after they've lost a loved one, if you have empathy, you can instantly envision yourself going through that same experience and feel what they are going through. Is it any wonder that "empathy" is an important key to unlocking the power of "kindness" in your life?

I imagine the empathy key as double hearts, entwined together. Empathy is the art of "knowing" someone so deeply that you feel what he or she feels compassionately and intimately. The more introspective, intuitive, and attentive you are to your feelings, the more you will be able to connect with the feelings of others. When you connect empathetically on such a deep and important level, you demonstrate over-the-top kindness, the kindness of letting down your defenses in order to truly "know" someone.

There's no doubt that our lives and our society could use large doses of empathy. It's obvious to see that our culture often prefers to dehumanize or demonize people rather than having a heart of empathy toward those who think, act, or believe differently than we do. In fact, having empathy is not only important when it comes to understanding others but it also compels us to take action to relieve another person's suffering.

Working through a prison ministry, I have done a lot of work with those who have been charged with felonies over the years. I meet people in prison and develop a relationship with them so when they get out, I can help them reintegrate into society. Often, they come out of prison with absolutely nothing. And to be frank, it's an uphill battle for such individuals to not wind up back in jail. It's hard for them to get a job because they don't have a phone, an ID, a social security card, and many of life's basic necessities. That's why part of our work is getting them set up at a halfway house for transitional living; then, we make sure they sign up for their driver's license, birth certificate, social security card, and other materials that they will need when looking for work. Finally, we help such individuals to get a job through a network of businesses and restaurants that we work with in the ministry.

Empathy is a big part of what I do in helping these inmates—both in prison and when they are released back into society. Often people won't look them in the eye or treat them fairly. In fact, too often, people dehumanize them, no matter what crime they committed. It's having a heart of empathy that enables me to see myself in their situation. By doing that, I can give them a sense of dignity and a sense of worth.

One of the things I love to do is take a newly released prisoner to lunch, either at their favorite restaurant, or to a place that serves their favorite food. When I meet somebody in prison, I always say to them, "When you get out, I'm going to take you to your first meal on the outside—anywhere you want to go, you pick whatever you feel like eating." I've kept this promise each time. As soon as one of them gets out of prison, I take them for a nice meal of their choice. It may seem a simple thing to do, but for ex-prisoners, it's a validation of both trust and affirming their worth and dignity as a human being.

WALK A MILE IN ANOTHER'S SHOES

"I do not ask the wounded person how he feels. I myself become the wounded person."

—*Walt Whitman, Song of Myself*

I love this Walt Whitman quote because it clearly articulates that empathy is walking in other people's shoes. So too, does the following story by S. Craig Glickman:

Several years ago, a young boy in Dallas was in an accident which necessitated the amputation of one of his arms. He withdrew from his family and friends and refused to talk to anyone. He was literally wasting away in withdrawal from life.

A friend of mine went to the hospital and asked if he might visit with the young fellow. This friend was met with skepticism but was allowed to visit the boy. When he came into the room, he saw the youngster staring out the window. The boy turned to see his visitor, who also lacked an arm. The boy looked at him for a few moments in silence. Then he said angrily, "You don't know how I feel, you couldn't."

"No, friend, you're wrong," the man said, "I do know how you feel. I also have lived without an arm."

The young boy hesitated a moment longer in his anger. Then he broke into tears as he ran toward my friend and put his one good arm around him. It was the beginning of the lad's recovery, which began when he found someone who really understood him.[24]

We all have difficult experiences in life. And often, God uses the very hardship, difficulty, or grief that we experienced to help others that are going through the same trial. I've heard Rick Warren say, "God never wastes our pain." The Bible says, "Praise be to the God and Father of our Lord Jesus Christ, the Father of compassion and the God of all comfort, who comforts us in all our troubles, so that we can comfort those in any trouble with the comfort we ourselves receive from God."[25] Empathy should be ingrained in the hearts and minds of believers. Our experiences in life, no matter how hard or horrible they may be, are a springboard for showing empathy to those we meet.

I know what it's like to lose everything. As I said in a previous chapter, when I lost my job, I literally lost everything. No paycheck. No benefits. No means whatsoever. We survived by getting food stamps and government insurance; utilizing churches' food pantries to get some groceries, and receiving the blessing and empathy of others who helped us and bought essentials for our family. I know what it's like to have very little and have a lot. And the Lord uses my experiences to help others who are dealing with the same situations I have had in life.

One of my favorite Bible stories is about the Good Samaritan. We don't know much about the man other than he was a Samaritan, but I've often wondered: had he ever experienced being robbed or

24.   S. Craig Glickman; used with permission.
25.   2 Corinthians 1:3-4 (NIV).

beaten at some point in his life? I wouldn't be surprised if he did. But the story is a glowing example of having a heart of empathy for people. Invest a moment to read it through:

But he wanted to justify himself, so he asked Jesus, "And who is my neighbor?"

In reply Jesus said: "A man was going down from Jerusalem to Jericho, when he was attacked by robbers. They stripped him of his clothes, beat him and went away, leaving him half dead. A priest happened to be going down the same road, and when he saw the man, he passed by on the other side. So too, a Levite, when he came to the place and saw him, passed by on the other side. But a Samaritan, as he traveled, came where the man was; and when he saw him, he took pity on him. He went to him and bandaged his wounds, pouring on oil and wine. Then he put the man on his own donkey, brought him to an inn, and took care of him. The next day he took out two denarii and gave them to the innkeeper. 'Look after him,' he said, 'and when I return, I will reimburse you for any extra expense you may have.'"

"Which of these three do you think was a neighbor to the man who fell into the hands of robbers?"

The expert in the law replied, "The one who had mercy on him."

Jesus told him, "Go and do likewise.'"[26]

GOING THE EXTRA MILE

The Bible says, "And if anyone wants to sue you and take your shirt, hand over your coat as well. If anyone forces you to go one mile, go with them two miles. Give to the one who asks you, and do not turn away from the one who wants to borrow from you."[27] Matthew 5:40-42-

Have you ever gone "the extra mile" for someone? Sometimes we go the extra mile at work—giving 110 percent—to impress our boss or to show ourselves worthy of a promotion. And I'm sure that many of us have gone "the extra mile" for our loved ones. But how often do we

26. Luke 10:29-37 (NIV).
27. Matthew 5:40-42 (NIV).

really go the extra mile for someone we barely know—a stranger, that person in need at church, that neighbor, or even our "enemy"?

Jesus' teaching on this really turned the scales upside down on how to love our neighbor. In the above Scripture, He tells us to go the extra mile for those who are suing us, not being kind to us, and to anyone who asks for something from us. The love of God is radical. It's inclusive—it's not a private club. This passage also shows us that no matter who the person is, we should go the extra mile to help them. Why? Because that's what Jesus does. His heart is loving and filled with empathy toward every human being. And that is the way He wants us to be as well.

Interestingly enough, I recently read an example of "going the extra mile" by a well-known company here in the United States. RitzCarlton co-founder and past president Horst Schulze said, "We are ladies and gentlemen serving ladies and gentlemen." Schulze's approach to the hospitality industry was "going the extra mile" for their guests. This included making sure that each guest was known by name. As soon as a guest was within earshot of staff, they were greeted by name. Schulze aimed for excellence in hospitality, treating guests and employees with the utmost respect and dignity. And, to Schulze, all staff were chosen not to merely serve but to show excellence to the customer. The grand effort into the details of a guest's stay became the earmark of the Ritz-Carlton. In fact, under Schulze's leadership, which took great strides to make sure that each guest was treated like royalty, the hotels earned an unprecedented two Malcolm Baldrige National Quality Awards and grew from four to forty US locations. Chick-fil-A has a similar "extra mile" philosophy for its organization.

How can you go the extra mile, especially for someone who is in a difficult place in their life? Besides paying someone a visit, sending a card with an encouraging note, or wiring a thoughtful gift, consider if there is a tangible way that you can help this person with their difficulty. Going the extra mile sometimes involves sacrifice on your part—if they need a place to stay, offer a room in your home. If they need transportation, let them use your car or offer to take them where they need to go. If the person is depressed or especially lonely, spend time with them and take them out on a fun outing. Showing empathy for a hurting soul is one of the kindest things you can do.

EMPATHY = LISTENING TO PEOPLE

"Most people do not listen with the intent to understand; they listen with the intent to reply."

—Stephen R. Covey, *The 7 Habits of Highly Effective People*

Most of us have no problem talking. But few of us are adept at listening. In fact, "listening" is increasingly becoming a "learned" experience. Dr. John Gottman, a clinical psychologist and relationship expert, highlights ten skills for active listening:

1. Focus on being interested, not interesting.

2. Start by asking questions.

3. Look for commonalities.

4. Tune in with all your attention.

5. Communicate you are listening with a nod/sound.

6. Paraphrase what the speaker says.

7. Validate the speaker's emotions.

8. Maintain eye contact.

9. Let go of your own agenda.

10. Turn off the TV.[28]

Listening is integral to relationships, and being able to truly listen to another person is at the core of having and showing empathy. Dr. Rachel Naomi Remen says, "The most basic and powerful way to connect to another person is to listen. Just listen. Perhaps the most important thing we ever give each other is our attention. . . . A loving silence often has far more power to heal and to connect than the most well-intentioned words."[29]

One area that I have found to be especially important is knowing how to listen to other people's needs. A friend from Facebook went

---

28. The Gottman Institute, https://www.gottman.com/.

29. Rachel Naomi Remen, *My Grandfather's Blessings* (New York: Riverhead Books, 2001).

through a difficult time in life. He was down on his luck. One day I was scrolling through Facebook and noticed that he had posted an image of a guy holding a sign that says, "Will write for food." At first glance I thought it was his "writer-humor" at work. But when I read his post, he said that he was looking for a fresh start and somebody that would take him in and help him out until he got back on his feet. I immediately messaged him, and said, "Hey, if you are serious, you're welcome to come stay with us. My son's away at college and we have an empty guest room."

When he came to stay with us, I learned that through a series of difficult life circumstances, my friend had found himself down on his luck. He had been living in his car and even on the street because he had nowhere to stay. I did a lot of listening to my friend's story, and my heart was moved with compassion. I didn't ask him why he had not told me about his situation. Instead, I listened, I loved, and I attended to his needs.

After six months at our home, my friend landed a job. He left our home renewed and ready to take on the world. Just a few days after my friend left, we welcomed into our home a traveling nurse who was waiting for his house to sell. We knew it would be a lot of money for him to stay in a hotel for one or two months, so we were happy to have him live with us instead.

Listening to people's stories and their needs is the first part of extending empathy and care. If we are willing to listen to others, God will surely open doors to enable us to make a difference in people's lives.

EMPATHY IS MOST PRONOUNCED WHEN WE SHOW UP FOR PEOPLE

"Nobody cares how much you know, until they know how much you care."

—Theodore Roosevelt

Have you shown up for somebody recently? Empathy plays a big role in showing tender care for people. My wife, a nurse, is an expert in empathy. She was led to her career choice because of her desire to help and care for people. Over the course of her professional life, she has seen so many hurting people and families—those who needed a huge dose of empathy, compassion, and loving care. A challenging but essential part of my wife's job is being a hospice nurse. When she sees the families of the loved ones placed in hospice, they are already at "the end of their rope" when it comes to their energy, emotions, and mental exhaustion. They have been caring for their loved one with a terminal illness, and now, there is nowhere to go but to hospice. Hospice is a death sentence. It's the end of the line, so to speak. They know that their beloved family member is going to die. It may be a week, a month, or three months, but they know they won't recover from it.

This is the atmosphere when my wife meets both the dying patient and their family. It's a very sensitive situation and usually tense at first. Sometimes the family members get really upset, rude, or snap at the nurse or the doctor because they're under such stress. So, empathy and grace play a massive role in what she does daily. In these difficult situations, my wife has genuinely come to see that the best thing she can do is show up—simply be there for the patient and the family members. A warm gesture, a comforting smile, and even an embrace help people know she cares.

I think sometimes we can over-complicate what it means to show empathy—to genuinely care about a person. Many times a hurting soul just needs your presence, even if it's simply a matter of you putting your arm around their shoulder and sitting with them in silence.

How do you empathize with loved ones, friends, co-workers, and family? Do you take the time to visit one of them when they are feeling blue? Do you surprise them with a meal or a treat when they aren't feeling well? Have you sent them a gift or even funds to help out in a time of need? Most of all, do you take the time out of your busy schedule to just be present with someone who could really use a dose of empathy and tender-loving care?

My wife's the type of nurse that when somebody is in pain, she's going to do whatever she can to get them the medicine they need. She waited at a 24-hour pharmacy until 2:30 a.m. to pick up a drug for somebody who needed it that night. And she literally took it to the patient in the wee hours of the morning so they could be relieved of their pain. Not only that, it was New Year's Eve. Yes, my wife came home, crashed, and was exhausted from the extra-long shift, but she slept like a baby knowing that her patient could finally have some relief from their pain and find some peace.

Just as we talked about going the extra mile for people, sometimes that includes inconveniencing yourself so that someone else can find a little peace.

THE EMPATHY OF JESUS

"Jesus wept."

—*John 11:35 (ESV)*

Jesus was filled with compassion, love, and empathy toward people. He even wept when He saw the grief, sorrow, and suffering that impacted people from sin, disease, death, and just the fallen condition of this world.

Jesus, indeed was empathy defined. He took time for people—the very people that the religious leaders shooed away. Time and again, the Lord looked at the throngs of people following him and the crowds that gathered to hear what He had to say and had great compassion for them. He said they were like sheep without a Shepherd. He knew each one of them. They were not faceless masses to Jesus. He knew each and every heart. He knew what each person was going through. And He knew what each person needed. Jesus always had tender words for the lost, hurting, rejected, and marginalized. He saved his harsh words for the religious leaders, who should have been good shepherds to the people, but instead were pushing people away from God by their rules, regulations, and hard hearts. Jesus had compassion when he saw the people and when he saw the crowds.

One of my favorite stories in the Gospels is this one:

A few days later, when Jesus again entered Capernaum, the people heard that he had come home. They gathered in such large numbers that there was no room left, not even outside the door, and he preached the word to them. Some men came, bringing to him a paralyzed man, carried by four of them. Since they could not get him to Jesus because of the crowd, they made an opening in the roof above Jesus by digging through it and then lowered the mat the man was lying on. When Jesus saw their faith, he said to the paralyzed man, "Son, your sins are forgiven."

Now some teachers of the law were sitting there, thinking to themselves, "Why does this fellow talk like that? He's blaspheming! Who can forgive sins but God alone?"

Immediately Jesus knew in his spirit that this was what they were thinking in their hearts, and he said to them, "Why are you thinking these things? Which is easier: to say to this paralyzed man, 'Your sins are forgiven,' or to say, 'Get up, take your mat and walk'? But I want you to know that the Son of Man has authority on earth to forgive sins." So, he said to the man, "I tell you, get up, take your mat, and go home." He got up, took his mat, and walked out in full view of them all. This amazed everyone, and they praised God, saying, "We have never seen anything like this!"[30]

Notice the great empathy the men had for their paralyzed friend. They were determined to help him, and they knew that the best help they could get was to bring their friend to Jesus. The crowds were so large that these men could not get close to Jesus by going into the house. But instead of giving up, their compassion and empathy for their friend spurred them on. So they literally started to take the roof apart so they could lower their paralyzed friend down, right in front of Jesus. Now that's a good friend. Jesus' response was one of great compassion and empathy. He didn't get mad at this riley group of friends who had just put a hole in the ceiling. Instead, He commended them for their great faith. And in doing that, He healed the paralyzed man, forgiving him of his sins.

Notice who in the crowd did not have empathy for the paralyzed man—the religious leaders. Instead, they were condemning Jesus for what He said. So, Jesus told the paralyzed man, "Get up, take your mat and walk."[31] And that's exactly what the young paralytic man

---

30. Mark 2:1-12 (NIV).
31. John 5:8.

did. Jesus healed him and all were amazed. Maybe God is going to heal your friend by seeing your faith and your heart of empathy to want to restore them and get them back on their feet.

Key Eight

UNLOCKING PATIENCE

How to Become a Person of Patience

"It is better to be patient than powerful. It is better to win control over yourself than over whole cities." Proverbs 16:32 (GNT)

It's always been said, from the time that I can remember, that it is dangerous to pray for patience. How could anything we pray for be "dangerous"? What this saying really means is when we are aware of our impatient nature and ask God to change us into patient people, He will bring situations or difficult people into our lives to teach us to be patient. Instead of being hasty, we learn the value of waiting on Him. We begin to understand that offenses aren't always personal. We realize that it's better to give people grace than a piece of our mind. And finally, the *aha* moment: when we love others as we love ourselves, we embrace the virtue of patience.

As we reach into our toolbox for our last few keys, we must pull out the key that unlocks our sense of patience. I imagine this key looks something like an hourglass. As we watch the sand pour thinly through the glass, we get a sense that time slows down. In a sense, that's what patience does for us—slows us down, takes us away from the "now" of immediacy, the insecurity of urgency, the demand to be served. Patience teaches us the kind of slowed-down awareness we need in order to truly pay attention to ourselves, God, our surroundings, and the people we are meant to connect with. Unlocking patience helps us to access our kindness potential in big and meaningful ways.

WHY UNLOCKING PATIENCE IS A CRITICAL KEY TO BEING KIND

"Patience is when you're supposed to get mad,
but you choose to understand."

—*Anonymous*

What is patience? According to the dictionary, it is the capacity to accept or tolerate delay, trouble, or suffering without getting angry or upset. I personally like dictionary.com's definition of patience. It says that patience is the quality of being patient, as the bearing of provocation, annoyance, misfortune, or pain, without complaint, loss of temper, irritation, or the like. I can really relate to this definition. Especially, the "or the like," which is a fill-in-the-blank answer. No one is immune to being impatient. We all have those moments. But, living a lifestyle of being impatience, or as I like to call it, having a short fuse, is a detriment to being a kind person. Impatient people are not kind people. That's why unlocking patience in your life is a key to releasing your kindness.

When I think about kindness and patience, they work in tandem. If you're short with somebody, you're certainly not patient. And when you're blunt with someone, you come across as rude, not kind. I've certainly been guilty of this.

I've been under a lot of strain lately, dealing with a difficult situation in our home while also being under pressing deadlines with my work, so I fired off a quick email the other day. After I sent it, I thought, "Oh, I hope they don't read anything into it or think I have a bad tone." I was honestly just trying to get it done quickly. But when you're short with somebody, you can come across as unkind. I was thankful that the person I emailed didn't think anything of it. Yet, I'm sure you have experienced impatient people in your life who have been anything but kind. Why is "patience" an elusive thing to grasp?

WHY ARE WE SO IMPATIENT?

Have you ever heard the phrase, "I want what I want when I want it"? Though it's been around for a long time, I think it's relevant to the technological and digital world that we live in today. We are accustomed to getting things quickly—whether it's a product, a meal, correspondence, or other deliverable.

Some of us remember when we had to save our money to get the product we wanted. Though financing large products (cars, homes, appliances, etc.) has been around for some time, we are now accustomed to financing everything, from the latest phone to even our pets. There are many apps and financial offers that allow you to pay installment payments on anything—whether it's a trip to a department store, shopping online, or staying at a vacation rental. We no longer have to save up for even small items. The motto of our age is, "Have whatever you want now. Or, as Burger King says, "Your way, right away." Another big hindrance to patience is the blessing (and curse) of living in a digital world. We can communicate with anyone and everyone around the world instantly. Whether it's texting, Snapchat, email, DMs, messaging, Zoom, or social media, we often expect an instant response and, more times than not, we get it.

You send an email in the morning, and by 5 p.m., you're nervous and thinking, "Why haven't I heard back from that person? They got my email *hours* ago." It's even worse now with texting. Because when you text somebody, they say texts have a 90 percent open rate—texts are opened and read at that incredibly high percentage rate. In full transparency, if I text somebody and they don't text me back almost immediately, I'm thinking, 'Hey, what's going on? I know they saw my text; why aren't they texting back?'

The ease and quickness of consumption, buying, and communication has made our human propensity to be impatient even worse. Most of us don't have to wait very much in our lives, and when we are required to wait, we not only feel inconvenienced but mistreated.

In full disclosure, I'm having my own bout with impatience right now. At the time of authoring this book, I'm having some intense health issues. The process of waiting on medical tests to be scheduled, test results to come back, and the litany of waiting for answers from doctors are getting to me. An example of this is I have a high white blood cell count, and I'm wondering what is wrong with me. I can't just see any doctor, I must see a hematologist oncologist, which is nerve-racking in and of itself. In trying to schedule an appointment, they are booked and can't see me for two months. I must wait two months to see if I have cancer or an infection? If I have an infection, shouldn't I be on antibiotics now? And if I have cancer, the earlier the treatment, the better. Why do I have to wait so long? It's testing my patience in a major way.

In the same way, my wife's stepdad was just diagnosed with ALS, which is also known as Lou Gehrig's disease. It's a terrible prognosis—giving a two-to-four-year life expectancy. To be sure of the diagnosis, the doctor wanted us to also see an ALS specialist for a second opinion, yet we couldn't schedule an appointment until two months later. That's a long time to wait when you're trying to find out if you or your loved one has a terminal disease.

Besides the instant access and gratification that pushes our patience level to minimal, there is something deeper inside of us that serves as the root of our impatience.

WHEN SELFISHNESS RULES, PATIENCE DOESN'T

Like so many of our weaknesses in life, the root problem that drives us to be impatient is our own selfishness. I'm not talking about the times when we need to get somewhere quickly because of an emergency (such as taking a child to the doctor), and something is delaying us. Instead, I'm talking about the kind of impatience that is a result of having our lives (including the people in our lives) and the world be the way we think it needs to be, *right now.* Impatience grows from a selfish thought process that makes our way, our needs, our desires, and our way of looking at things the dominant concern. The intensity of our impatience tells us how much we think we need to achieve our own agenda *rather than* following God's agenda and timing for our life.

Bottom line? When we put ourselves on the throne instead of God, we are not only impatient about everything and everyone but are clearly showing a lack of love for others as well.

WHAT DOES A PATIENT PERSON LOOK LIKE?

"I will not be distracted by noise, chatter, or setbacks. Patience, commitment, grace, and purpose will guide me."

—Louise Hay

What does a patient person look like to you? When someone once asked Dallas Willard to describe Jesus in one word, he said, "Relaxed." Man, I had to chew on that for a while. It cuts me to my core in today's busy culture to reflect on this. I believe the perfect picture of patience would be found in Jesus' time on earth. He never rushed anywhere. In fact, He often took the "long way around" to encounter certain people at specific times. He walked miles and miles with His disciples, tarrying at various locations and ministering to people everywhere He went. Jesus was on God's timetable. He waited patiently, knowing that God's timing was always the right timing. There are many examples in the Gospels of Jesus saying, "It is not yet my time." Jesus' agenda was His Father's agenda, not His own. The Bible says, "For I have come down from heaven, not to do My own will, but the will of Him who sent Me. This is the will of the Father who sent Me, that of all He has given Me I should lose nothing but should raise it up at the last day."[32]

Jesus is the perfect model of what patience looks like. When you're following God's agenda, rather than your own, you have perfect peace in waiting on God's timing. In Jesus' economy, delays are God-sent. Please read that again, friend.

One of my favorite stories in the Gospels is when Jesus raises Lazarus from the dead. Mary, Martha, and Lazarus, who were siblings, were very good friends of Jesus.' When Lazarus got extremely ill, Mary and Martha sent a messenger to find Jesus and tell Him to come right away. When the messenger found Jesus and His disciples, Jesus told him to tell Mary and Martha that He would come to see them and Lazarus.

---

32. John 6:37-39 (ESV).

But Jesus did not leave immediately. In fact, it took several days for Him to get there. When Mary and Martha saw Jesus and His disciples coming up the road, Martha ran to Jesus and with tears flowing, said, "Lord, if you had been here, my brother would not have died."[33] Why did Jesus wait? Didn't he love Lazarus and his sisters?

When Mary and the rest of the village ran out to Jesus and showed Him where Lazarus had been entombed, Jesus wept. The Bible then tells us, "So they took away the stone. Then Jesus looked up and said, 'Father, I thank you that you have heard me. I knew that you always hear me, but I said this for the benefit of the people standing here, that they may believe that you sent me.' When he had said this, Jesus called in a loud voice, 'Lazarus, come out!' The dead man came out, his hands and feet wrapped with strips of linen, and a cloth around his face. Jesus said to them, 'Take off the grave clothes and let him go.'"[34]

Jesus could have rushed to get to the village and healed Lazarus before he died. But God had a greater plan than healing. Jesus patiently waited because He knew that He was going to do a greater miracle—bring Lazarus back to life.

HOW OTHER PEOPLE BENEFIT FROM OUR PATIENCE

When we are patient toward others, they benefit from it because we are showing them grace—which is a gift of unmerited favor. Besides love, grace is something every single person needs. When I show my kids patience, I show them grace. Let me ask you, is there anyone in your family who needs grace from you?

When I show patience to somebody in my life, it's always met with appreciation. There's nothing my wife hates more than to feel rushed. It was a point of contention early on in our marriage because I always told her, "Let's go, let's go." Of course, it only took me like five minutes to get ready, and I struggled to see what took her so long. But I finally learned that there was a big difference between how I got

---

33. John 11:21 (ESV)
34. John 11:41-44 (NIV).

ready and what she needed to get ready. It taught me to be patient, and she has always appreciated (and even thanked me) for not rushing her.

Showing patience to others makes a difference in their lives. We all need grace—we all need people to extend grace to us. It's far better to show patience to your loved ones than to be absorbed with your own agenda. Remember, unlocking patience is the key to showing kindness to others, and the best place to practice this virtue is right at home with your own family.

PATIENT TOWARD SOME, BUT NOT OTHERS?

Have you ever noticed that it's easier to be patient with some people but difficult with others? Sometimes it's easier to be patient with those who have been through so much in their lives. It's also easier to be patient with someone you have a relationship with versus a stranger—whether they be someone standing in line at a store or someone on the road.

I believe for many people, the biggest challenge in showing consistent patience and grace is with those in their own families. The reason for that is because these are the very people we are around the most and that we "do life" with daily. My wife and kids require more patience from me and vice versa. It's the reality of doing life together. When we are in community with others, which includes church relationships too, we must be intentional about being patient consistently and generously.

PATIENCE SHOULD BE EVIDENT IN CHRISTIANS

Patience is not a "suggestion" for Christians. Instead, patience is one of the earmarks of a Christ follower. The Bible says, "But the fruit of the Spirit is love, joy, peace, patience, kindness, goodness, faithfulness, gentleness, self-control; against such things there is no law."[35]

---

35. Galatians 5:22-23 (ESV).

When believers walk with Christ, they are to bear the fruit of the Spirit. As you see by the verse above, this includes patience (and notice kindness is there, too). Now, as human beings, we don't always get it right 100 percent of the time, but a true Christ follower will practice patience more than not. It's going to be a part of our daily life, especially in our own homes.

There are times in life when God uses situations and people to refine our character and make us more like Christ. I have personally found that "patience" is one of those tools that the Lord uses. It's interesting that the Bible also uses the word "longsuffering" when it talks about being patient. I love the word "longsuffering." It's more descriptive than "patience." When someone is long-suffering, it means they patiently endure lasting offense or hardship. Or, as I heard one pastor say, "We suffer long."

Do you suffer long? Is your patience long-lasting or does it give out after a few times? The Bible often refers to God as being long-suffering with us. He's slow to anger—he bears with us as we stumble and fall through life. God is not waiting for you to blow it so He can pounce on you. Quite the opposite. He is patient and gracious toward us. And because He is long-suffering, His mercies are new every morning.

There is power in showing kindness. If there's a situation where the natural human response would be impatience and rudeness, but I come across with grace and kindness, it surprises people and takes them aback. I had one person say to me, "Wow, I was a jerk to you, and you responded so kindly—I'm really surprised."

Patience, like kindness, is a mark of a Christ follower. And the more we show these virtues to others, the better our world will be.

LOVE IS THE FOUNDATION
FOR PATIENCE

"Love is patient and kind; it is not jealous or conceited or proud; it is not arrogant or rude."

—1 Corinthians 13:4 (ESV)

If you say you love someone, or that you're a loving person, but you aren't patient or kind, then you aren't showing love at all. At the end of the day, each of the keys to kindness in this book comes down to love. If you love someone, you're going to be patient with them—you're going to be kind. But if you're short-fused, angry, jealous, conceited, selfish, and arrogant, you simply are not loving them.

As a former pastor and counselor, I can tell you straight up, it all begins in your own home. Your kids and your spouse need your patience and grace– they need the foundation of love to undergird everything you do. When love starts with God, and flows through you to your family, you will find that it flows easily to others as well.

Does kindness win over selfishness in real life? Consider this interesting true-life story:

> President William McKinley was once planning to appoint an ambassador to a foreign country. There were two candidates whose qualifications were almost equal, and McKinley searched his mind for some yardstick by which he might measure the true greatness of both men. He later confided that the self-centeredness of one man and the magnanimous kindness of the other man were the deciding factors in his choice.
>
> See, many years before, when McKinley was still a representative in Congress, he had boarded a streetcar at rush hour and got the last vacant seat.
>
> An old woman entered shortly afterward carrying a heavy bucket of washing. She walked the length of the car and stood in the aisle, hardly able to keep her balance as the vehicle swayed on its journey. No one offered her a seat.
>
> One of the men the future President was later to consider was sitting opposite where she was standing. McKinley noticed that he shifted his newspaper to avoid seeing her.
>
> McKinley walked down the aisle, took her basket of washing, and offered her his seat in the back of the car. The candidate never knew that this little act of selfishness had deprived him of perhaps the crowning honor of his lifetime. Indeed, the President later remembered this unkindness and decided to appoint the other man as his ambassador.[36]

---

36. This President William McKinley anecdote was adapted from Paul F. Boller Jr., *Presidential Anecdotes* (Oxford: Oxford University Press, 1996).

Key Nine

UNLOCKING LOVE

How to Love Ourselves, Love Others, and Love God

"Love cures people—both the ones who give it and the ones who receive it."

—*Karl Menninger*

The work of the Menninger Clinic is organized around love. "From the top psychiatrist down to the electricians and caregivers, all contacts with patients must manifest love." And it was "love unlimited." The result was that the hospitalization time was cut in half. There was a woman who for three years sat in her rocking chair and never said a word to anyone. The doctor called a nurse and said, "Mary, I'm giving you Mrs. Brown as your patient. All I'm asking you to do is to love her till she gets well." The nurse tried it. She got a rocking chair of the same kind as Mrs. Brown's, sat alongside her, and loved her morning, noon, and night. The third day the patient spoke, and in a week, she was out of her shell—and well.

WHAT IS LOVE?

"Love is more than a noun—it is a verb; it is more than a feeling—it is caring, sharing, helping, sacrificing."

—*William Arthur Ward*

Philosophers and intellectuals have been trying to define "love" for centuries. When you open a dictionary, you get a simplistic definition that says, "an intense feeling of deep affection; a great interest and pleasure in something." Pretty inadequate definition, isn't it? In fact, I believe all the definitions over the centuries fall short of describing what "love" truly is—except for one: the Bible.

As a pastor, I've done many weddings over the years. And I always like it when the "love" chapter in the Bible is read and shared in the ceremony. If you have never read it, take a moment, and read it here: "Love is patient and kind; love does not envy or boast; it is not arrogant or rude. It does not insist on its own way; it is not irritable or resentful; it does not rejoice at wrongdoing but rejoices with the truth. Love bears all things, believes all things, hopes all things, endures all things. Love never ends."[37]

It's an incredible definition of love. Too often, we relegate love to a romantic definition or classify love, like the dictionary does, as a "good feeling." But love is far more than a feeling or a romantic relationship. Love is a bond that is found in all kinds of relationships, and it is also a way of living. You see, love is more than a noun. Love is a verb as well. And when love is your main motivation, your actions show it.

The above Scripture about love is not only a great definition, but it is also a great meter to check how well you love. Muster up some courage and give yourself a test. Reread the Scripture passage above. But this time, where the word "love" is written, replace it with your name instead. For example, in the first sentence, when I replace "love" with my name, it reads:

> "Greg Atkinson is patient and kind; Greg does not envy or boast; he is not arrogant or rude."

Now it's your turn. Go ahead and put your name and pronoun in place of "love" and "it" in the following:

> "[Your name] is patient and kind; love does not envy or boast; [he/she] is not arrogant or rude. [He/She] does not insist on [his/her] own way; [your name] is not irritable or resentful; [your name] does not rejoice at wrongdoing, but rejoices with the truth. [Your name] bears all things, believes all things, hopes all things, endures all things. [Your name] never ends."

---

37.   1 Corinthians 13:4-8 (ESV).

So, how did you do? Do you feel like you didn't score very high on the love meter? Don't worry, you are not the only one. This little exercise really does open our eyes to what love is and how we don't measure up as much as we want to. However, don't despair. We can learn to love like this. No, we will never be perfect, but we sure can come closer to really living a lifestyle of love.

With only two keys left to go, this one is vitally important. If any one of our keys can effectively open wide the fences that divide and bind us, it's the key to unlocking our love. This key, in the shape of a heart, allows our love to flow openly from us into the world. It dispels hate and apathy, immobilizes self-critique, and releases us from all that binds our spirit. If you want to access your true potential for kindness, you must unlock your ability to love and love well. Maybe you are wondering how in the world we can love like this. The key is found in knowing the author of love.

THE GREAT COMMANDMENT OF LOVE

"When I have learnt to love God better than my earthly dearest, I shall love my earthly dearest better than I do now."

—**C.S. Lewis,** *Letters of C. S. Lewis*

Understanding that God's very nature is love will transform your life. F. B. Meyer once said, "The love of God toward you is like the Amazon River flowing down to water a single daisy." That's how great God's love is toward you and me. And Jesus is the greatest example of God's love in action. The Bible says, "In this the love of God was made manifest among us, that God sent his only Son into the world, so that we might live through him."[38]

George Mueller was an incredible man of faith. He and his wife ran an orphanage and depended upon God for every meal and every need that they had in life. They continually took in children who were left on the streets to die. Their great love for the children in their care flowed from their great love for God. One of my favorite

---

38.   1 John 4:9 (ESV).

quotes from Mueller is simple but profound. He said, "It matters to Him about you."

You matter to God. I think those are the four most beautiful words I've ever heard. And when you come to the full understanding that the very author of life loves you with such a deep love—a sacrificial and unconditional love—you just can't help loving Him back.

WE CAN FULFILL THE GREATEST COMMANDMENT

When we know God's love, our focus should be on loving Him back. One of the most well-known Scriptures in both Judaism and Christianity is called The Great Commandment. It is recorded for the first time in the Old Testament, and then repeated by Jesus during His earthly ministry.

"But when the Pharisees heard that he [Jesus] had silenced the Sadducees, they gathered together. And one of them, a lawyer, asked him a question to test him. 'Teacher, which is the great commandment in the Law?' And he said to him, 'You shall love the Lord your God with all your heart and with all your soul and with all your mind. This is the great and first commandment. And a second is like it: You shall love your neighbor as yourself. On these two commandments depend all the Law and the Prophets.'"[39]

We need to love God first, above everything and anyone else. It is God's love flowing through us that motivates our love for Him. That's why the great commandment is to "love the Lord your God with all your heart (your thoughts, feelings, inclinations, and understanding), with all your soul (your very breath, spirit, self), and with all your mind (mental power, might, strength).

While on staff at Transformation Church in Charlotte, Dr. Derwin Gray, the Senior Pastor, taught the Great Commandment a bit differently than what I'd heard throughout my Christian life. I had always heard we were to love God and love people—a two-prong approach. But Dr. Derwin Gray taught a three-prong approach

---

39. Matthew 22:34-40 (ESV).

regarding love. The first and most important prong of the Great Commandment is upward—we love God first. The second prong is inward – because God loves us and we love God, we can then love ourselves. And the third prong is outward—we love others. So, upward, inward, and outward.

This teaching of the Great Commandment opened my eyes. I'd never heard the part about if I don't love myself, I can't properly love others. All I ever heard was love God and love people. We totally missed the love ourselves part. Yet, when you look at the Scripture passage in Matthew 22, it is clear that we are to love our neighbors as we love ourselves.

Until you really love yourself, you're not going to be able to love others in a healthy way. *This truth has radically changed my life . . .*

LOVING OURSELVES NEEDS TO BE IN THE MIX

Why is loving ourselves important? If you don't properly love yourself, you certainly aren't going to love others well. Instead, you will walk around in a bad mood, angry, upset, short with people, blunt, and rude toward others. Just as we all know that "hurt people hurt people," it is also true that "loved people love people."

Many people, rather than loving themselves, struggle with self-hate. They can't seem to forgive themselves. They may say they forgive others. They may say they forgive their dad. They may say they forgive the person that abused them. But they don't forgive themselves. They are their own worst critics. They don't like who they are, and that impacts how they perceive others, and certainly how they treat others.

You need to forgive yourself. And you need to understand that because God loves you, you can indeed love yourself. And when you let God's love flow through you, motivating you to love God with all your heart, soul, and mind, you will find that you can love yourself, and in turn, love others in the same way.

LOVE ONE ANOTHER . . .

"These things I command you, so that you will love one another"

—John 15:17 (ESV)

When Louis Lawes became prison warden of Sing Sing Correctional Facility in 1920, the inmates existed in wretched conditions. This led him to introduce humanitarian reforms. He gave much of the credit to his wife, Kathryn, however, who always treated the prisoners as human beings. She would often take her three children and sit with the gangsters, the murderers, and the racketeers while they played basketball and baseball.

Then in 1937, Kathryn was killed in a car accident. The next day her body lay in a casket in a house about a quarter of a mile from the institution. When the acting warden found hundreds of prisoners crowded around the main entrance of the prison, he knew what they wanted. Opening the gate, he said, "Men, I'm going to trust you. You can go to the house." No count was taken. No guards were posted. Yet not one man was missing that night. Love for one who had loved them made them dependable.

How does Christianity show up in the world? Is it through politics or culture wars? Jesus said that the world would know that we are His followers when we love one another. That is the measure of following Christ. That is our witness. And that is how the early church turned their world upside down for God—through love.

LOVE IS A VERB

Love is not static—it's always moving and doing for others. And it's a foundational motivation in showing kindness to one another.

A popular viral trend today is Random Acts of Kindness, where various people are paying it forward in a variety of ways. You see it on Instagram, TikTok, and more. I mentioned earlier in the book about Keanu Reeves who is habitually reaching out to people in creative acts of kindness.

There are many ways that you can show kindness. Have you ever picked up the tab for someone at a restaurant? When going through a drive-thru, have you ever paid for the car's meal behind you? My daughter once worked at Dunkin' Donuts, and she said one day, there were about twenty cars in a row that paid for each other in line—they just kept it going and going. I've had that happen to me at Dunkin' Donuts and Chick-fil-A. And I've been in restaurants where I go to pay the server, and the waitress says, "Somebody already picked up your meal."

One of the most incredible ways to show the love of Christ to others is by *doing* something for them. Do you know a family that might be struggling financially? Take them some groceries, give them a gift card, or take them out to dinner. I knew of a well-off lady who helped a single mom at her church by filling the oil tank in their home so they had heat for the winter (that's for all the East Coast people reading this).

There are many ways to show love through random acts of kindness. You don't need money to be kind. How about visiting an elderly person or shut-in neighbor you know? Do you know someone who is battling cancer? Offer to go with them to one of their chemo appointments. Maybe you know a busy and worn-out single mom who could use some rest or time to herself—offer to watch the kids so she can get some rest or be able to go shopping alone.

As believers, especially, we need to have our eyes open to the needs of others. Loving people in tangible ways goes far in showing them just how much God cares about them.

HAVING AN "OTHERS FIRST" MENTALITY

The Bible says, "Do nothing from selfish ambition or conceit, but in humility count others more significant than yourselves. Let each of you look not only to his own interests, but also to the interests of others."[40] How do we follow an others-first mentality?

---

40.   Philippians 2:3-4 (ESV).

Jesus' ministry on earth was "to serve and not be served." Now, think about that for a moment. He wasn't just a regular man. Yes, he was fully man, but He was also fully God. And He said, "Whoever has seen me has seen the Father."[41] In other words, everything Jesus said and did was representative of God the Father. So, if Jesus had a "servant's heart" that means God has a "servant's heart." That reality should blow your mind. It sure did mine.

I believe one of the best examples of humility and servanthood is found during the Last Supper. It's the night before Jesus' arrest, and He and His disciples were gathered together to share the Passover meal in the upper room (what would be Jesus' last meal before His crucifixion). The Bible says, "[Jesus] rose from supper. He laid aside his outer garments, and taking a towel, tied it around his waist. Then he poured water into a basin and began to wash the disciples' feet and to wipe them with the towel that was wrapped around him."[42]

It was common in the Middle East that a servant would wash the feet of the guests entering a house because their feet would be dirty from their travels. Remember, besides an animal here and there, walking was "the" mode of transportation. And the terrain that people walked through was sand, dirt, and mud. The role of washing people's feet was reserved for the "least" on the social ladder. But here's God, taking the humblest of positions, serving His disciples by washing their feet. Jesus said, "Even the Son of Man did not come to be served, but to serve, and to give his life as a ransom for many."[43]

So, as Christ-followers, we are to serve one another; to esteem another higher than ourselves, and to love another with the love that Jesus shows us. There have been a lot of great books written on servant leadership over the years. When I took on the mantle of leadership at the age of eighteen, I had to learn to serve first. And in all that I do, both personally and professionally, for the past three decades, stems from the model of servant leadership.

So, to have an others-first mentality, you have to intentionally practice daily to choose to love others—to treat them as you would

41.   John 14:9 (ESV).
42.   John 13:4-5 (ESV).
43.   Mark 10:45 (ESV).

want to be treated. When you know you are loved by God, and that He Himself is a servant leader, it gives you the foundation to love others.

DOING LIFE TOGETHER—LIVING IN COMMUNITY

At the root of loving and serving others is the fact that we are in relationship with people. Christianity, the way of life that we have adopted as Christ followers, puts us in relationship with God, and in relationship with others. We're not going to stay alone in our house, like a hermit. Instead, we are going to live, work, and play in relationship with others.

My wife and I decided to start a new small group, something popular in many Christian churches where people meet in someone's home and develop friendships and encourage one another on life's journey. It's an intentional action to "do life together" rather than just flying solo.

Pastor Andy Stanley of North Point Church has said that life happens in circles, not rows. In church, you have rows of seats or pews. But life happens in circles when you're in a small group with one another—you're looking in each other's faces and sharing your story, struggle, pain, and prayer requests. That's where true ministry happens. I see this all the time, and in recovery groups as well.

Everything comes down to relationship. We have a choice whether we want to be in relationship with others. I've said for years that ministry is people. And we shouldn't be in ministry if we don't like people. So I have intentionally chosen to be in relationship with people—all kinds of people. If I haven't heard from somebody in a long time, I will pick up the phone and text or call them. Too many people wait for someone to reach out to them instead of being intentional and taking steps to reach out to others.

Listen, God didn't mean for us to do this life alone! Don't live in a silo; esteem others above yourself, reach out to people, serve others, and you will find that life is much more than just living for yourself.

WHEN WE LOVE OUR ENEMIES, WE SHOW THE HEART OF GOD

"Love your enemies, do good to them, and lend to them without expecting to get anything back."

—Luke 6:35 (NIV)

During the Revolutionary War, there was a faithful gospel preacher by the name of Peter Miller. He lived near a fellow who hated him intensely for his Christian life and testimony. In fact, this man violently opposed him and ridiculed his followers.

One day the unbeliever was found guilty of treason and sentenced to death. Hearing about this, Peter Miller set out on foot to intercede for the man's life before George Washington.

The general listened to the minister's plea but told him he didn't feel he should pardon the minister's friend.

"My friend! He is not my friend," answered Miller. "In fact, he's my worst enemy."

"What?" Washington said. "You have walked sixty miles to save the life of your enemy? That, in my judgment, puts the matter in a different light. I will grant your request."

With pardon in hand, Miller hastened to the place where his neighbor was to be executed and arrived just as the prisoner was walking to the scaffold. When the traitor saw Miller, he exclaimed, "Old Peter Miller has come to have his revenge by watching me hang!" But he was astonished as he watched the minister step out of the crowd and produce the pardon that spared his life.

Loving your enemies can be very difficult, especially if they have hurt you or a loved one badly. I've heard stories over the years where parents of children who have been sexually abused or even murdered have forgiven the offender.

One story that hits home for me is when on June 17, 2015, nine people were shot and killed inside Mother Emanuel AME Church in Charleston, South Carolina. Not only do I live in South Carolina, but I went to college in Charleston and lived there eight years. My son goes to the College of Charleston and lives just one block from Mother Emanuel. So, this tragedy really hits close to home for me. After the shooting, the killer appeared in court the next day. According to the *Washington Post*:

> One by one, those who chose to speak at a bond hearing did not turn to anger. Instead, while he remained impassive, they offered him forgiveness and said they were praying for his soul, even as they described the pain of their losses.

> "I forgive you," Nadine Collier, the daughter of 70-year-old Ethel Lance, said at the hearing, her voice breaking with emotion. "You took something very precious from me. I will never talk to her again. I will never, ever hold her again. But I forgive you. And have mercy on your soul."[44]

When we hear stories like that, we may scratch our heads and say, "How in the world can they do that?"

Personally, I think apart from Christ, it's very difficult. However, as Christ followers, there are a few things we need to remember about God's treatment of us, and our responsibility to give out what we have been given. For example, the Bible says, "For if while we were enemies we were reconciled to God by the death of his Son, much more, now that we are reconciled, shall we be saved by his life."[45]

I think one of the reasons we can love our enemies, even when they've committed a hideous crime, is because God loved us when we were still enemies toward Him. And when Christ, who was innocent, suffered unbearable beatings and torture, ending with the His brutal death of crucifixion on the cross, He continued to love humanity. In fact, while dying on the cross, He had compassion on his killers (and all us sinners), saying, "Father, forgive them, for they know not what they do."[46]

---

44. Mark Berman, "'I Forgive You.' Relatives of Charleston Church Shooting Victims Address Dylann Roof," *Washington Post*, June 19, 2015, https://www.washingtonpost.com/news/post-nation/wp/2015/06/19/i-forgive-you-relatives-of-charleston-church-victims-address-dylann-roof/.

45. Romans 5:10 (ESV).

46. Luke 23:34 (ESV).

Loving our enemies comes down to the recognition that just as God loved us while we were shaking our fists at Him, then we too are to love those who are shaking their fists at us (so to speak). Another way of saying it is, just as Christ has forgiven us of all our sins, so must we forgive those who have sinned against us. Since God has not withheld His love or forgiveness from us while we were sinners, neither shall we withhold love or forgiveness from those who are sinning against us.

The Bible says, "If your enemy is hungry, give him bread to eat, and if he is thirsty, give him water to drink, for you will heap burning coals on his head, and the Lord will reward you."[47] When you are kind to somebody that hates you, it confounds them. It singes their conscience, even if they don't show it.

I have had some people that have betrayed me or treated me poorly throughout the years, and I have to say, it is hard to want to do good to them. I think this is something that most of us struggle with. But part of the Christ follower discipleship journey is trying to live in Christ's love toward others, including our enemies. Though it's tough, it is an effort worth making. First, it really does show the love of Christ when we can love our enemies—and it can go far in bringing that very "enemy" to Christ themselves. Second, when we truly forgive our enemy (which means not holding the offense toward us against them), it sets us free. It goes back to the idea that choosing to live is better than being bitter. When we refuse to forgive someone, we become bitter, which chokes out the love of Christ working in our lives. It is far better to love our enemies, no matter what they have done, than live a life in bondage to bitterness and hate.

There is too much hatred in our world. When we choose to love God, ourselves, and others we are not only living a beautiful and powerful life but empowering others to find freedom in Christ and live in love as well.

---

47. Proverbs 25:21-22 (ESV).

UNLOCKING UNITY

How to Bring Unity into Your Life and Make the World
a Better Place

"There are three ways to ultimate success: The first way is to be kind. The second way is to be kind. The third way is to be kind."

—Fred Rogers, a.k.a Mister Rogers

Imagine a world where everyone is kind to one another . . .

Imagine a world where people go out of their way to treat others just like they want to be treated themselves . . .

Cast a vision of how your life would change—how your relationships would change—just by being kind to those you work with, live with, socialize with, attend church with, and live in the neighborhood with . . .

Just imagine . . .

You made it to the last chapter, and perhaps you are wondering, "Greg, in such a volatile and divided nation and world, can one person's acts of kindness really make a difference? After all, it seems like Christians can't even agree or get along. In the grand scheme of things, does all this really matter?"

Without reservation, I can honestly tell you, yes, it really does matter. Too often, we think that we, as individuals, don't have the power to make change in our world. But the reality is that every good thing—every good movement—starts with one person.

For those of you who are reading this book and are Christians, I might add that a small cadre of Jesus' followers (powered by the Holy Spirit, of course) turned the world upside down (even the powerful Roman Empire was impacted by the early "church").

Yes, one person can make a difference. Simply put, being kind is how you, as a human being, contribute to society and make the world a better place.

There is no doubt that our world is in turmoil. And, more than we have ever known, there is deep division in our communities, churches, nation, and across the globe. That's why the last key to kindness is found in unlocking unity.

As you pick up this last key out of your toolbox, take a deep breath. When you unlock this last padlock restricting your soul, you may feel a rush of fresh air as the gate swings open. Opening ourselves up to connection, to unity, frees us in ways we cannot imagine. In a sense, we are opening our hearts to give and receive not only kindness but true meaning and bonding as human beings with ourselves, each other, and the world we live in. Often we can fall for the illusion that self-sufficiency and independence will make our lives better. But kindness emerges instead from relationship, connection, and interdependence. Shaped in the form of a triple-circle, this last key embodies the very spirit of the Trinity. The more connected we are with God, ourselves, and others, the more our potential for kindness will empower us to be authentic healers and world changers.

DIVIDED WE FALL—THE NEED FOR UNITY

"Only humility will lead us to unity, and unity will lead to peace."

—*Mother Teresa*

There is a beautiful Hebrew legend of two brothers who lived side by side on adjoining lands. One night, the older brother lay awake and thought, "My brother lives alone. Unlike me, he doesn't have the companionship of a wife and children to cheer his heart. While he sleeps, I will carry some of my sheaves into his field." (Sheaves are a bundle of grain stalks tied together after reaping.)

At the same time, the younger brother, who lived alone, thought, "My brother has a large family, and his necessities are greater than mine. While he sleeps, I will put some of my sheaves into his field."

Thus, the two brothers went out, each laden with sheaves—and met at the dividing line of their properties. There they embraced. Years later, at that very place stood the Jerusalem temple, and on the very spot of the meeting stood the temple's altar.

I love the story above. Two brothers, thinking of the greater good of the other, come together at the "dividing line." And that very spot—where they thought more highly of the other's needs than their own—would end up being the place upon which the great Jewish Temple would be built. Friend, that is the heart of kindness that leads to unity. And that is exactly what our families, workplaces, communities, nation, and world need right now.

In all my years (and I've got grown kids, so I've been around for a pretty long time), I've never seen the extent of division that we are experiencing today in our society. Some analysts have said that we are broaching on (or near) the equivalence of bitter division that was found in the United States prior to the Civil War. Sadly, we are divided over:

- Politics

- Race

- Social justice

- Morality

- Diversity

- Human rights

- Human dignity

- Faith

- And so much more . . .

105

Though there have always been dividing lines and tensions when it comes to politics and beliefs, I have not witnessed the level of incivility and hatred toward one another like I see today. Our divisiveness has not stayed in the political arena; it has invaded our lives, dividing friendships, families, and, sadly, even our places of worship. We are too quick to judge, cancel, and hate one another instead of striving to come together and find solutions—to even try to get along. That is why it is so important to understand that unlocking unity in our lives is the key to kindness. There is strength in unity, and it unleashes the power of kindness in our own homes, communities, and nation. Seeking a spirit of unity means we humble ourselves and start listening to those who think or believe differently than we do.

I have a friend by the name of Chan, a sixty-plus-year-old Asian woman whom I've known for many years. She works in the service industry, owning a mid-size salon, and we have great talks about all sorts of subjects. Chan is friendly, kind, and loving, but she has been faced repeatedly with racism and has been treated very poorly. So, she put a sign in her office saying, "Please Be Respectful." This poor woman has encountered clients that have been mean, rude, and, yes, racist. When I told her I was writing this book on kindness, she said, "Oh, that is so important. The world needs a book on kindness. Please tell people to be kind to those of us in the service industry."

We need more kindness in America instead of being offended and arguing about everything. You would think the pandemic would have united us, but instead, we argued about wearing a mask or not wearing a mask, taking the vaccine or not taking the vaccine, and whether churches should be open or closed.

Why can't we unite over the horrible atrocities that many of our African American neighbors have experienced, rather than being offended when someone says, "Black Lives Matter?"

Many of us grew up watching Mr. Rogers. He was an incredible man who taught us to be kind, polite, and respectful. Fred Rogers was ahead of his time when it came to matters of racism and social justice. On one of the episodes of "Mr. Rogers' Neighborhood," he invited his friend, a Black police officer, to put his feet in the kiddie pool along with his own so they could cool off on a hot day. They both took their socks and shoes off and put their feet in the pool together, something that was unheard of in that day and time. In fact, it was ground-breaking. And though some people were shocked, it was a moment in history where Mr. Rogers showed others what it means to love their neighbor, no matter what their skin color may be. Fred Rogers' kindness was a catalyst in showing unity during a time of deep division.

That's what we need today. We need to show unity by showing kindness to our neighbor, no matter who they are—whether they are a different race, faith, gender, sexual orientation, or hold different beliefs and have different politics.

Martin Luther King Jr. said, "We must learn to live together as brothers and sisters or perish together as fools." It's time we all start learning to live together—and being kind to one another is a great first step.

IN A CHURCH DIVIDED, JESUS CALLS FOR UNITY

"Every kingdom divided against itself is laid waste, and no city or house divided against itself will stand."

—*Matthew 12:25 (ESV)*

Throughout the history of the church, there have been times of division, reformation, and restoration. After all, though Christ is the head of the church, human beings comprise it—which means sometimes we don't always act according to the Spirit, but rather, more like our sinful nature. The deep divisions we see in our country have not escaped the church. Sadly, and indeed sometimes, instead of bringing healing and unity we have just brought more division.

Now, to be fair, divisions in the church have gone back to biblical times. Often, the arguments have been centered on theology, Christian practices, and even style of worship. Followers of Jesus span the globe. In fact, there are more than 2 billion Christians throughout the world.[48] That's quite a phenomenal number of Christ fol-

---

48.   Pew Research Center, "Global Christianity—A Report on the Size and Distribution of the World's Christian Population," Dec. 19, 2021, https://www.pewresearch.org/religion/2011/12/19/global-christianity-exec/.

lowers. Yet, these 2 billion faithful people are separated into 45,000 denominations globally.[49] Why so many different denominations? It all comes down to theological differences, and often these differences are not about the major tenets of the faith (though some are) but more about what we pastors would call the *nonessentials* of the faith—those things we can agree to disagree on without breaking fellowship together. Yet, too often instead of unifying, we separate off into our own denomination to be with people "like us."

The bottom line is if we as the church can't get along, how are we all going to get along as a community, as a nation, and as a global people?

JESUS' HEART FOR UNITY

Jesus knew, right from the beginning, our human propensity to argue and divide into groups (and cliques, I might add). The Lord had a burden for His church to be united, and He prayed for this very thing before He died on the cross:

> "I do not ask for these only, but also for those who will believe in me through their word, that they may all be one, just as you, Father, are in me, and I in you, that they also may be in us, so that the world may believe that you have sent me. The glory that you have given me I have given to them, that they may be one even as we are one, I in them and you in me, that they may become perfectly one, so that the world may know that you sent me and loved them even as you loved me."[50]

Did you notice that Jesus said, "our love and our unity" will show the world that God sent Jesus because He loves humanity? It is through the love and unity of Christians (the church) that the world will know Jesus.

One of the most well-known Bible verses says, "For God so loved the world, that He gave His only begotten Son, that whosoever

---

49.   Donavyn Coffey, "Why Does Christianity Have So Many Denominations?" Feb. 27, 2021, Live Science, https://www.livescience.com/christianity-denominations.html.

50.   John 17:20-23 (ESV)

shall believe in Him, will not perish, but have eternal life."[51] Again, in Jesus' prayer, He says, "That they may become perfectly one, so that the world may know that you sent me and loved them even as you loved me."

Our greatest unifier in the church should be the Gospel—John 3:16. It is through our love for one another and our unity that the world will know we are "the real deal" and that the Gospel is true.

THE WAY OF CHRIST

Believers are to present a right representation of Christ. We are to model the way of Jesus—His very character, His teachings, and His love, grace, and mercy toward humanity. If we don't model it correctly, we're not the salt and light that God called us to be in this world.

Sadly, in our society today, Christians are more known for their politics. We can show hate rather than love toward people. And too often, we seem angry and judgmental instead of forgiving and gracious.

We need to exile the political definition of Christian and get back to the true definition, which is "little Christ," meaning Christ followers. That is the original translation of Christian in Scripture. The early church followed the way of Jesus—they lived and modeled Christ, who was humble, meek, kind, gracious, loving, and merciful. Jesus ate with the sinners and loved the hurting and broken people who were ignored by the religious leaders of the day.

The apostle Paul said, "Imitate me, just as I imitate Christ."[52] We are to follow Christ and abide in Him, meaning that as we stay close to Jesus and follow His way, we will walk in the Spirit and our lives will be characterized by love, joy, peace, patience, kindness, goodness, faithfulness, gentleness, and self-control.

I love how Fred Rogers, a.k.a Mister Rogers, puts it when he says, "Try your best to make goodness attractive. That's one of the toughest assignments you'll ever be given." The goodness of Christ is

---

51. John 3:16 (ESV).
52. 1 Corinthians 11:1 (AMP).

attractive when we are walking in the Spirit and bearing the fruit of His characteristics, as I've listed above.

I had a mentor in high school named Jerry Stepp. He helped me get into college, audition for a scholarship, and took me under his wing. I was an intern at my church, and Jerry would take me to visit nursing homes, shut-ins, and those in hospitals. I was doing all this at the ripe age of 16, but Jerry knew that it would give me the heart of God for hurting people. To this day, Jerry is the kindest person I know. I always say he has the fragrance of Christ. Whenever I am around him, it feels like I'm hanging out with Jesus because he is so kind, loving, and accepting of people. That's what the church needs today. We need to be followers of the way of Jesus, living and walking in the fruit of the Spirit and emitting a sweet aroma to all those we encounter.

WHAT THE WORLD NEEDS NOW
IS KINDNESS

"Be kind, for everyone you meet is fighting a harder battle."

–Ian Maclaren

There is power in kindness. Margaret Cho once said, "Sometimes when we are generous in small, barely detectable ways it can change someone else's life forever." She's right. Steve Sjogren, who is an author and a friend, once made an astute observation about Cho's comment. He wrote: "Margaret Cho is referring to the butterfly effect of kindness. It's small, doable acts of practical kindness that shape the world."

You can genuinely make a difference in someone's life by showing them kindness. Everybody faces a battle in their life—we need to remember that. When you see someone in a store, at a restaurant, or at a medical office that seems rude or has rubbed you the wrong way, instead of getting irritated or angry, pause for a moment and consider what they may be going through in their life. And then, shower them with kindness—a big smile, a compliment, calling them by their name—which can go a long way in lifting their spirit, encouraging their heart, and giving them hope in life. Yes, that's just how powerful kindness can be.

I was talking to my landscaper the other day when he came to cut the grass. And sometimes he can be a little difficult or rub me the wrong way. But I was telling him that I just got out of the hospital due to heart issues. We had a nice conversation. Now, he didn't tell me what battle he might be facing, but the odds are there is something he's dealing with in his own life. He could be going home to a toxic situation, or he may have a kid with special needs, or he may have his own medical concern. We simply don't know what people are facing in their lives, so being kind to everyone we meet, whether they are nice or curt, can be the healing balm they need.

I grew up being taught by my mom how important it was to be polite, to have manners, and to treat people with respect. I think sometimes we have too readily discarded these teachings as "being old-fashioned." But being kind should never go out of style. And having manners and being polite is not only a part of being kind but also a simple way to show people respect. I was taught to say "yes, ma'am" or "yes, sir" or "no, ma'am" or "no, sir." I was also taught to thank people on a regular basis. I'm tremendously grateful that my mom taught me manners and raised me to be polite. She would take me along with her when she helped people, or, did "Meals on Wheels," or when she taught the Sunday School class for the elderly. I always saw her serving people. One of the simplest but most appreciated acts of kindness my mom did was providing meals for people who just got home from the hospital, or for those who were sick and alone at home. There's no doubt that church people do this well.

Be creative in extending kindness to people. Treat all you meet with respect and dignity. When you do, remember what Anne Frank once wrote, "How wonderful it is that nobody need wait a single moment before starting to improve the world."[53] The simple acts of kindness go a long way in healing people's hearts and lives.

REMEMBER GOD'S KINDNESS

53.   Anne Frank, *The Diary of a Young Girl*, reprint ed. (New York: Bantam, 1997).

111

TOWARD YOU

The following is a Scripture that I've held dear for many years and have spent a great deal of time reflecting on: It is "the kindness of God that leads us to repentance."[54]

It's God's kindness that leads us to repentance. He's not the angry man upstairs throwing down lightning bolts. So, what draws us back to God when we stray? It's his kindness. That's the gracious God we serve, and who we model our lives after as Christ followers. We serve a kind, gracious, and loving God. His love for us is unconditional. He showers us with unmerited favor. And His mercies toward us are new every morning.

There's a myth out in the world that the Old Testament God was mean, angry, and upset, while the New Testament God is gracious, loving, kind, and merciful. It's as if we think that God has a split personality or just changed into a kinder, gentler being over time. But that is far from the truth. The God of the Old Testament and the God of the New Testament are one in the same—and both show the character of God's kindness and love toward us.

There are numerous (too many to count) Scriptures in the Old Testament that show how kind God is toward His creation. I love the story of Jonah because it reveals just how kind God is and just how opposite humans can be. Jonah was told to preach to the people of Nineveh, who were the worst of the worst sinners. They were not kind people, to say the least. God wanted the Ninevites to repent, so He sent Jonah to them to preach. But Jonah didn't want to go. He hated the people of Nineveh, and quite frankly, he didn't want them to repent. After stewing in the belly of the whale for three days (that's another story for another time), Jonah finally did what God asked him to do and went to Nineveh and preached for them to repent.

And do you know what happened? The Ninevites repented and returned to God, but Jonah got upset because he wanted them wiped off the face of the earth. Hmmm . . . do we see this kind of behavior today among some of our churches?

---

54. Romans 2:4 (NASB).

Jonah said to God, "I knew this is what you were going to do. I knew you were kind. I knew you were gracious and merciful." God's character has been consistent all throughout Scripture. He's always been loving and kind. You can see from Jonah's example that our natural selves have more of an inclination not to be kind. But being kind and loving our neighbor flows out of our walk with God. It's the byproduct—the fruit—of spending time with God. The more time we spend with Jesus, the more we take on His character traits of love, kindness, grace, and mercy.

The world needs true Christ followers—people who love Jesus and love their neighbor, no matter who they are or what they believe. Look at your neighborhood, your community, and your own family and relationships. Are they seeing the love of Christ in you?

There is no doubt that we need to show more kindness towards one another. Consider for a moment each of the ten keys of kindness that we have covered in this book:

1. Forgiveness
2. Generosity
3. Composure
4. Acceptance
5. Rest
6. Wisdom
7. Empathy
8. Patience
9. Love
10. Unity

Now imagine unlocking each of these keys to kindness and living your life loving your neighbor in this way. . . .

When you walk in kindness toward others—forgiving them, being generous to them, having composure toward them, accepting them, being at rest with them, showing wisdom towards them, having a heart of empathy for them, being patient with them, loving them, and being a peacemaker toward them—it breaks down the wall of division and brings unity like nothing else can.

This, my friend, is the secret power of kindness—that you can be a part of a movement to change the world and make it a better place.

Will you join me in this great calling?

SCAN HERE to learn more about Invite Press, a premier
publishing imprint created to invite people to a deeper
faith and living relationship with Jesus Christ.